All
Nature
Sings

Library of Congress Cataloging in Publication Data

De Jonge, Joanne E., 1943–
  All nature sings.

  (My father's world)
  Summary: Twenty-three essays describe unique and
interesting facts about insects and other small animals which are
part of God's created order.

  1. Animals—Addresses, essays, lectures—Juvenile literature.
[1. Animals—Addresses, essays, lectures] I. Bishop, Richard, ill.
II. Title. III. Series.
QL49.D37   1985   591   85-7724
ISBN 0-930265-12-2

All Nature Sings

Joanne E. De Jonge

Illustrations by Rich Bishop

CONTENTS

ALL NATURE SINGS

We all sing about God's glory in nature. Phrases like "purple mountain majesties," "the lily white," and "the birds their carols raise" roll off our tongues with no trouble at all. Even this series of books takes its title from the song "This Is My Father's World." Nature is nice to talk and to sing about—"nice" nature, that is.

That's the problem. We sing only about "nice" nature. Somehow, in our minds, we've divided God's creation into two parts. There's the part we celebrate in song: purple mountains, white lilies, rustling grass, and caroling birds. That's the "nice" part, the part that shows God's glory, we think. Then there's the "other" part: the slimy slug, the hairy tarantula, the slithering snake. We know that God created these "creepies," but we certainly don't care to celebrate them in song. We don't sing about *all* nature.

Yet *all* nature does sing God's praise. That slimy slug tells us that God has a place for each of his creatures. The hairy tarantula shows by its actions that God gives even his small creatures perfect instincts. And that snake slithering through the grass displays God's wisdom in giving every creature a body fit for its lifestyle. Every lowly creature sings God's praises in its own way. We simply don't know the song.

Most of this book is devoted to that "other" part of nature and to hearing its song. It introduces you to my Father's slug, it examines that earwig on my toothbrush, and it listens to the crickets' late September serenade. It insists that if you know these creatures, you too will hear their song.

Because *all* nature sings, some other more "acceptable" animals have been included. Gerbils scurry over the back pages, Pat the porcupine waddles past, and a herd of yaks model their magnificent winter coats. The white lily and caroling birds are included in other books of this series.

One final word of encouragement to the fainthearted: Nothing will jump from these pages to bite you. This is, after all, a book and not a zoo. Even if these creatures were alive and at your fingertips, not one would harm you if treated with care and respect.

So don't skip immediately to the more "acceptable" creatures. Spend some time with the worms, the pillbug, and Harry's cobra. Become acquainted with those little creatures as well as the larger beasts. As you begin to understand them, perhaps you'll be able to hear their songs of praise. Then you'll realize that, certainly, *all* nature sings.

1

Loops in My Sweater

Two years ago I had a sweater I just loved. It was a white, lacy-looking V-neck, and it matched anything I wore. I could throw it into the washing machine, and it would come out looking like new. It was as comfortable as a bathrobe, but it always looked neat. I wore it all the time.

The only problem with that sweater was that it caught on everything. Its lacy pattern had lots of single threads. I was forever catching those threads on jewelry, music stands, and staples on bulletin boards. Anything that could possibly catch seemed to reach out and pull that sweater. Every time I planned to wear the sweater, I'd first have to turn it inside out and pull all the loopy catches to the inside.

One morning I was late for school. My trusty sweater went on in a hurry, before I pulled the catches inside. When I noticed some loops, I did a real "no-no." I took a scissors and snipped them all off. I knew, in the back of my mind, that I shouldn't do that. But the sweater looked fine. I couldn't see where the funny loops had been. No one noticed that a few strands were missing.

Then I washed the sweater. I was absolutely horrified when I pulled it out of the machine. It was full of gaping holes. In fact, it was more hole than sweater. It was absolutely unwearable. All those loops I had cut had been part of the pattern. They had held other threads together.

I couldn't bear to throw the sweater away, so I put it in my dustrag box. Every time I dust with it, I wish I could be wearing it instead.

Last spring, when we first returned to our cabin in the woods, we noticed that moles had been busy near our front door. What a mess they had made! Unsightly ridges and bumps on our yard marked their travels as they tunneled through the soil in their constant search for insects and worms.

As I walked into the woods again, the blue jays set up a ruckus. I was a little irritated at first. I had forgotten about all the noise they make. They definitely made me feel like an unwelcome guest in "their" woods. Sometimes I yelled back at them, but that didn't quiet them at all.

As I neared my favorite sitting tree, I noticed that a woodchuck had dug a hole right where I

used to sit. Dirt and sand littered the ground around the tree. Grudgingly, I sat down next to another tree.

As I sat, I was glad to see the red-tailed hawk glide silently between the trees. Apparently he was back. Hawk had made his home somewhere in our woods the year before. I had seen him swoop down to pick up a rabbit or a little mouse. I had always felt a little sorry for the unfortunate creature that didn't get away.

I also noticed that tent caterpillars were there again. Tent caterpillars show up in our woods every spring. They make such a mess in the trees when they make bigger and bigger tents. Our neighbor destroys every tent he can find in his woods. We simply put up with them. They're messy, but they disappear eventually.

During our first night back at the cabin, a skunk woke us up. This had happened the year before also. We never heard the skunk; we woke up from the odor. I think that the smelly skunk traveled right under our bedroom window. It probably went to the river to hunt for turtle eggs.

I rolled over and muttered, "The skunk's still here," and wished it had chosen a path farther from the cabin.

Before I fell asleep again, I started thinking about that skunk. I began to realize that it was sort of like one of those loops on my white sweater.

I didn't want the skunk there. It was a nuisance sometimes, and I would almost wish that it weren't there. But if the skunk weren't around, there would probably be far too many turtles by the river. They would eat all the frogs, snails, and tiny fish. Then the raccoons and 'possums wouldn't have enough food. They too eat little water creatures.

The tent caterpillars were also like loops on my sweater. If I cut them out, I'd be cutting off the food source of some beetles. I'd also be cutting away the moths that hatch and visit our woodland flowers. And the goldfinches that nest near the edge of the woods would have to find other nesting materials. They often use the old tents of these caterpillars.

The red-tailed hawk is another necessary "loop." If it didn't catch rabbits and mice, our woods would be full of these little creatures. Both multiply rapidly over the summer. Too many rabbits and mice would eat too many leaves and too much grass. They would deprive deer of food. So we need the hawk if we want the deer.

The big, old woodchuck is a very obvious "loop." I can't miss where it's been. But if it hadn't been there, soil in the woods wouldn't be mixed and wouldn't be nourished by its food and its droppings.

Even the blue jays stick out like loops on my sweater. But they serve a purpose, even if I don't always like it. They *do* warn others of my coming, and I *am* an intruder in the woods.

And those moles with their unsightly tunnels—surely they're some of the biggest "loops on my sweater." But they also help let air and water into the soil. And all those grubs and insects they eat? If all of them lived, our woods would be in real trouble.

By the time I fell asleep, I had mentally pulled in all the "loops on my sweater." The skunk, tent caterpillars, hawk, woodchuck, blue jays, and moles all belonged in the woods. You see, the woods is rather like my white sweater. It's one big fabric made of many small threads. If one thread is cut, the whole fabric suffers.

There's one big difference, however. I can recycle my old sweater into a dust rag and buy a new one. But I can't make a new woods.

2

This Is My Father's Slug

"Of course we appreciate nature," you say. "Don't we even sing about it? 'Of rocks and trees, of skies and seas, His hand the wonders wrought.' "

Every time we sing that song I have an impish urge to change the words. One of these days I'll sing at the top of my voice, ". . . of bats and bugs, of snakes and slugs, His hand the wonders wrought."

I wonder what the reaction around me would be. Probably shocked silence. Who would ever sing about slugs?

We're funny that way, you know. We praise God for a wonderful creation and shudder at some of his creatures. We have dozens of songs about rocks and rills, purple mountains, and fields of ripened grain. I've never heard even one verse about the slimy slug.

What can be said for the slug, that snail-without-a-shell? Something that slithers on a slimy trail, feeds mostly in the evening or after a rainfall, and hides in dark, damp places must be up to no good. That mucus-covered, formless blob seems to have no redeeming features. Actually, it seems to have no features at all.

I'm talking about the common garden slug, the brown or black blob you see chewing up your lettuce or lurking about your lawn. Its cousins, the sea slugs, are often dressed in beautiful purples, lavenders, or white-with-red-trimmings. However, the landlubber slug we're considering has not been blessed with anything that might endear it to us.

Maybe slugs don't care whether or not they're endeared to us. Bright purple or lavender probably would be very easy to see on a lump of dark soil. Maybe the garden slug has its dark, unexciting color for protection. It does blend well with the soil.

That slimy coat is really great protection. The mucus keeps the slug moist and comfortable. It also forms a gluey mess that discourages predators and people from meddling in the slug's affairs. Sometimes the mucus may even contain poison to convince animals that slugs don't make good suppers.

A slug not only lives in slime, it also travels on

it. A small gland, the pedal gland, sits above the slug's one foot. This secretes slime and lays it down ahead of the foot so the slug can glide smoothly about its business. Scratchy sand, dry grass, and hard concrete all become one super-smooth highway under the slug's little gland. A slug can even travel safely over the business end of a razor blade. Now, that's effective slime!

Formless as a slug may seem to you and me, it really contains most of the organs we possess. A two-chambered heart pumps slug blood. A lung cavity, a liver, a crop, a kidney, a stomach, and slug-type intestines work just fine.

Like its cousins, the snails, a slug has a pair of eyes, complete with lens, cornea, and retina. They're even set far out on a pair of tentacles that can be pulled in, away from danger. Another pair of tentacles helps the slug smell and feel danger and food. A rasping, file-like tooth-tongue combination scrapes up food as the slug glides on its merry way.

For food the slug may select the lettuce in your garden. It may also select a small rodent that has died in a nearby field, or a heap of decaying vegetation. You see, most slugs are scavengers. They eat dead and rotting plants and animals. In so doing, they're performing a service for us. As bits of plants and animals pass through a slug's body, they're broken down to still smaller bits and passed on to still smaller scavengers. Eventually these plants and animals are broken down completely and returned to the soil as nourishment for plants.

I'm sure that slugs don't think about this as they eat. They're just acting according to instinct. But I'm sure that God thought about it when he made a slug. After all, this is my Father's slug.

3

Don't Kill a Scutigeromorph

I lived in the tropics several years ago, before I knew anything about the natural world. Any creature I didn't recognize I suspected of having evil intentions toward me. I thought anything that crawled, especially if it had six legs or more, should be promptly eliminated. I was constantly doing battle with "those funny things" whose hot, humid world I shared. However, there were many more of them than of me, so I didn't make much of a dent on their populations.

One particular incident often comes back to haunt me. I had found a centipede scooting across our living room floor boards. Armed with my can of "bug bomb," I gave chase, spraying half the can on it—in front of it, behind it, and above it. I can still see those long legs, wet with "bug spray," dragging through the puddle I had sprayed. I remember screaming hysterically, "It won't die! It won't die!" I think it finally drowned.

Had I known then what I later learned, I never would have given chase to that little centipede. It was probably there after our cockroaches.

Centipedes hide in dark, damp places and prey on slugs, worms, and juicy insects that live there. They work at night and avoid the light. The centipede I drowned probably had been disturbed under our house and had come up through a crack.

I know now that it was a scutigeromorph, a long-legged centipede that is sometimes found in houses. I also know that some people welcome them because they keep insect populations in check.

The centipede's first pair of legs is a specially formed set of hunting tools. It's a pair of poison claws that can pierce the centipede's prey and inject poison.

If left to its own devices, a centipede prefers to use those claws on insects. It may, however, use it on a human that disturbs it. I'm told that a centipede's bite is like a wasp sting. Most house centipedes are considered quite harmless, if treated right.

The rest of a centipede's legs—fifteen pairs—are very long. This gives it tremendous speed in running down prey. The little scutigeromorph has been clocked at 50 centimeters (19.7 inches) per second. That's 3,000 centimeters, or 1,182 inches, or 99 feet, per minute!

A centipede is flattened from top to bottom, so it can scoot into little cracks and under stones. It has tiny eyes but uses its antennae more when searching for prey in its dark world.

Besides having a body built to fit into damp, dark cracks, a centipede seems to have two special senses that help it survive.

It has a special light sensor in its skin. Even if it is "blindfolded," it will avoid light and scurry into the darkness whenever it can. This helps the centipede stay under cover, where it is protected from enemies and from drying out.

It is also very sensitive to touch and seems to "want" as many parts of its body as possible in contact with something solid. This generally keeps it in little cracks, out of the sight of animals and humans with "bug bombs."

Some female centipedes lay their eggs in soil and then leave them. Others are the picture of motherhood.

One of these motherly centipedes will lay a cluster of eggs and curl her body tightly around them so that they cannot be seen. If an eggs falls out of the cluster, she'll pick it up and put it back. Occasionally she will unwind, pick up an egg and lick it. She doesn't really have a tongue, but she cleans the egg with her mouthparts. Naturalists believe she is removing spores of molds that might grow on the egg and kill it.

I haven't been able to find out if scutigeromorphs are a kind of centipede that cares for its eggs. But I have found out a lot about centipedes and other things that crawl.

I have found out that most of the creepers and crawlers I see belong where I find them. Most of them are designed for a certain task, which they perform well. And if I find them out of place, they're usually more afraid of me than I am of them. Even in the tropics, I learned, all those "creepies" belong.

If you see a low-slung flat "thing" with many legs scuttling around, it's probably a centipede. If it's brownish and has fifteen pairs of very long legs, don't kill it. It's probably a scutigeromorph, and it's probably just looking for a dark place and a juicy insect.

4

Scorpions

I knew by the way it crunched that it was a scorpion . . . or had been. That crunch was one of a scorpion's defenses cracking beneath my bicycle tire. With its hard skin broken, the scorpion—or whatever it was—might not live long.

I didn't get off my bike to check. It was dark, and I wasn't about to step anywhere near a scorpion with only flip-flops on my feet—especially if the scorpion were dying. It might just be a little angry. I know that *I* would be, if someone rode over me with a giant bicycle. I too would probably lash out at anything that came near me. So I just muttered, "Sorry," and kept right on going. In fact, I got out of there in a hurry.

I was fairly sure that it was a scorpion, anyway.

I had seen its shadowy form just before I rode over it, but I had thought it was a stick. It was long—probably over five inches. That's long for a scorpion. They run anywhere from one to six inches. In temperate climates, like ours in North America, they may be an average of three inches or so. But I was in a tropical climate, and they grow things big in the tropics.

I knew that other big creepies were out and about on tropical nights. Spiders grow to astonishing sizes too, but their shadows are roundish. This thing was long and narrow, like a cigar. Beetles grow big there too, but beetles don't have pincers like this thing had. I saw the pincers just before I heard the crunch. It could have been a lobster, but I was thirty miles from the South China Sea. So it was either a twig with claws or a scorpion. In the night shadows, it had at first looked like a twig to me.

Because it was night, the scorpion was out and about. Naturally quite shy and secretive, scorpions hide under stones, dead leaves, or rubbish, or in cracks and crevices during the day. And they hide alone. They don't like company, not even that of other scorpions. Only when night falls will they come out to hunt. And then, when bothered, they prefer to run and hide rather than fight.

Of course, this one hadn't had a chance to run and hide. I rode right over it before either I or it knew what was happening. A scorpion is no match for a bicycle. Yet I did wonder if it had

managed to sting my tire. All the rest of the way home I listened for the telltale hiss of a leaking bike tire.

Scorpions don't always use their stingers. That I knew. They have large, pincerlike claws that they hold in front of them. They use these to test the ground ahead and to capture their food. They use their stingers sometimes when their prey struggles. But mostly they use their stingers for defense.

Their curved stingers are at the end of their "tails" (which aren't really tails, but are part of their bodies). Two poison glands open into each scorpion's stinger. Usually a scorpion holds its "tail" curved over its body. If something threatens, the scorpion whips its "tail" foward and tries to hit that dangerous something with its poison stinger.

Usually a scorpion knows when danger is coming. It has eight to twelve simple eyes. Some are placed in front of its head and some on the sides, so it can see movement on three sides of its body.

Scorpions also have pectines, peculiar comblike structures that only scorpions have. These pectines are attached to their undersides and have nerves and muscles connected to them. We think that scorpions use their pectines to feel vibrations on the ground.

The scorpion I hit must not have been using its pectines. Or maybe it just didn't have a chance to react. After all, a scorpion—even a big one—is no match for a full-grown person on a bike.

I really didn't have to worry about my tires. I should have worried more about the scorpion. Suppose this were a mother scorpion with babies on her back? Maybe I had wiped out several scorpions with that one crunch.

Mother scorpions protect their young for a while. Young scorpions are born just that way—as young scorpions. They don't hatch from eggs. When they're born, they climb on Mama Scorpion's back and stay there for ten days to two weeks. After they've molted (shed their skin) once, they climb down. They may stay near Mom for a day or two but soon are off on their own.

Of course, chances were better that it was a single scorpion, but I still worried just a little. Not enough to go back in the dark and look, though. "Why worry about a scorpion, anyway?" I thought. "There are enough creepies around here."

And there were: huge spiders, enormous cockroaches, and big black things that buzzed when they flew and that both stung and bit. Lizards, geckoes, and snakes crawled in the grasses; and rats and mice grew larger, faster, and more numerous than I believed possible.

Of course, that's why scorpions thrive in that tropical climate. They love to eat all of the above creepers, crawlers, and buzzers. They help keep things in check.

Even here, in our temperate climate, they keep the same kinds of creatures in check. That's why they're here and that's why we'd worry if they weren't.

"Here" is mostly the southwest section of North America. In the northeast section and other places where scorpions don't live, something else lives to take their place. Where scorpions live, they are needed.

I guess I had an inkling that scorpions were needed in the tropics. That's why I worried just a little bit when I crunched that one with my bike. "Just a little bit" because I knew that there were others. One more or less wouldn't make much difference.

This meeting had been purely accidental. By mutual consent, scorpions and I stayed away from each other. I knew that they didn't care to meet me, but I didn't care to meet them either. I always faithfully shook out my clothes before I put them on and checked my bed before I crawled into it. I really didn't want to come into contact with scorpions, much less kill one.

Most scorpion stings are merely painful, like a wasp sting. But some are dangerous and deadly, especially to small children. That's why it's wise not to bother scorpions. A scorpion usually won't sting unless it feels threatened.

The scorpion I rode over was definitely threatened, but it didn't sting. It didn't have time. My bicycle was too fast. Scorpions were created to do battle with other creatures, not bicycles.

I really did feel bad about riding over it. The whole thing was an accident, a fatality for the scorpion. I checked the next day. It was still there, dead. Too bad. I'm sorry.

5

A Million Lives

Yesterday I went outside to lie in the sun. I spread my blanket on the grass, me on my blanket, closed my eyes, and tensed every muscle in my body. I was waiting for that first ant to explore my exposed toes, that beetle to drop unannounced from the tree, or that spider to march across my stomach, and I could think of little else.

Three minutes later I still had no visitors, so my mind began to wander. Perhaps somehow I had caught all curious critters beneath my blanket. Perhaps, at that very moment, some were trying to bore through that blanket so carelessly thrown over their homes. More likely, they were scurrying frantically downward, trying to

escape the big thing that had blundered into their world and now lay on top of it. I began to wonder about just what did move beneath my blanket.

Earthworms, probably. I had read someplace that 190,000 earthworms can live in one acre of soil. Surely at least a few were burrowing beneath my blanket at that very moment.

If there were earthworms, there just might be a slug or two. Some slugs like to eat earthworms. A slug could be down there, stretching itself through a burrow in search of an earthworm.

There were probably quite a few roundworms, or nematodes. One bucket of soil can house millions of those tiny, thread-like worms. Perhaps millions wiggled beneath my blanket, feeding on bacteria, algae, and tiny soil-animals.

A millipede or two may have scuttled into the soil when it felt me coming. Millipedes can burrow through soil; they often do so to escape a hungry mouse or bird.

I wondered if the soil was moist enough for springtails, tiny insects. Those that were at the surface may have sprung away. Other slightly different springtails live within the first few inches of soil. Still others live deeper down. Surely there were some springtails beneath my blanket.

I couldn't forget the spiders. I knew I hadn't blundered into a web, but I may have spread the blanket over a trap door. Some spiders tunnel into the ground and build a trap door at the entrance of the tunnel. Perhaps some spider was trying in vain to lift its trap door at that very moment.

There also must have been some mites feeding on decaying matter and soil-animals in the soil beneath me. I had heard once that hordes of mites live in the top few inches of soil. They're so tiny that we can hardly see them.

I may have covered a ground beetle or two that had burrowed its way into the soil. Or maybe a tiger beetle had been caught as it burrowed into the ground after prey.

Certainly I lay above a beetle larva or two, probably several. So many different kinds of beetle larvae wiggle within the soil that I couldn't begin to name them.

Perhaps a cicada larva was developing near the roots of that maple tree.

Maybe wire worms had worked their way below me and were attached to some tender root.

And how could I ever have forgotten the ants? Perhaps I had laid my blanket over an anthill. At that very moment an ant queen might be laying eggs down there. Workers were probably scurrying about busily. The ant colony down there might even have some guests, perhaps an ant beetle, a cricket, a silverfish, or a cockroach.

I began to think of everything happening in those few square feet of soil beneath me. Creatures were scurrying along rootways. Others were digging tunnels or hollowing out rooms. Some were resting, others were hunting, and still others were hiding from the hunters.

I remembered reading that a single footstep on soil will change millions of lives. Air pockets shrink, tunnels collapse, and plant roots are crushed. Hordes of creatures living in the pockets and tunnels or on the roots die. But millions more will be born or hatch, and thrive on the decay.

If one footstep can affect so many creatures, I wondered, what does one body carelessly sprawled out on a blanket do? I rolled over and thought, "A million creatures ruined, but a million more supplied with food."

I had never really considered life in the soil before that. I had never realized that one little patch of earth was so full of life.

I began to itch and tickle, imagining a million little creatures creeping and crawling over me. Finally I got up, folded my blanket, and went inside.

6

Worms

We went out digging for worms a few days ago. It's easy enough to do if you know how. You put the shovel or pitchfork into the ground, wiggle it a while, and out pop the worms. You have to be sure a worm is all the way out of the hole before you snatch it; else you might have a tug of war and end up with half a worm in your hand while the other half wiggles back down into the soil.

I've dug, or "wiggled," for worms like that many times before and often ended up with only half a worm, but I never really thought about it much. Someone had told me long ago that a worm will grow a new half if it's pulled apart; and besides, it's only a worm, so why worry about it?

The other day I started thinking about it.

Those poor little worms really pull back when you try to pull them out of their holes. They must have some kind of feelings. What do they pull back with? They feel so slippery, you'd think that they'd just slide right out of their holes. Will an earthworm really grow another half? If it does, it must be quite a complicated little creature. Then how can anyone possibly say it's "only a worm"?

I've done a little investigating since then and found out some very surprising things about earthworms.

An earthworm feels slippery because it has the soft, moist body it needs to live in moist soil and to burrow in snug little tunnels.

If you pull an earthworm through your fingers from the tail end forward, you'll find that the body really isn't smooth; on each little segment there are eight tiny bristles. The worm can move these bristles forward or backward like little legs, to help it crawl through the soil. It can also hang on tightly to the soil with these bristles when someone tries to pull it out of its burrow.

A worm will grow a new back half if it's pulled apart. If you're ever digging worms and happen to pull one apart, please be sure you put the front half back. The front half is a little bit too complicated to grow back. You see, the front of an earthworm contains a crop, or storage place, for its food, and a gizzard with heavy muscles to help digest the food and to pass it on to the intestine in the back. The brain is in the front, connected to a long nerve cord that runs to the back. Earthworms have five pairs of hearts in the front that pump blood through blood vessels. They also have egg sacs in the front part of their bodies.

Did you ever wonder what that one smooth band near the front of an earthworm was for? It's called the clitellum, and it has a very special purpose. When an earthworm has mated, the clitellum makes a gelatin ring. This ring moves toward the front of the worm, gathering the worm's eggs as it moves. When it slips off the worm's head, it forms a cocoon, keeping the eggs safe until they hatch, in about three weeks.

When worms burrow into the ground, they often swallow the soil, getting a good part of their meals that way. By burrowing and eating soil, worms stir and mix it and bring deep soil to the top. Since they cannot swallow stones, and since the soil they eat is fine, coarse soil is gradually buried. All soil that passes through a worm's digestive system is enriched.

The little pellets of earth that worms bring to the surface are called castings. Worm castings help bury dead plants and seeds. Dead plants enrich the soil more and seeds sprout and grow.

Worms' tunnels let air and rain seep into the soil, keeping the soil full of oxygen and moisture.

Worms also pull little plants beneath the surface of the ground to keep the soil rich and spongy.

When top layers of the soil become dry in the summer, worms burrow deeper down. In the winter, worms plug their tunnels and go deep again. Some worms can live for about twelve years, staying in surface soil when conditions are right, and burrowing deep down if it gets dry or cold.

If there weren't any earthworms, the earth would probably be hard, growing only a few scraggly plants. Trees would be smaller. Grass would be less healthy, and animals that eat the grass would be less healthy. There would be less food for us and for animals. This world would certainly be a different place to live without worms—different, and not as nice.

Maybe that's why God made worms able to grow again if they're broken in half. Maybe he knew how important they'd be to us, and how little we would think of them. Maybe he knew how we'd look at them and say, "Oh, well, it's only a worm." Never again will I say that about this piece of God's creation.

7

Daddy Long-legs

A "spider" crossed my path last night. My first impulse was to step on it. After all, I was in a hospital at the time, and the spider was steering a course toward a patient's bed. Eventually it might get to the bed and cause some alarm. Should I step on it? I went to the sink and washed my hands while I thought about it.

This "spider" was a daddy long-legs, and I've always been told that they do no harm. Once in a while one may catch an insect or two, but usually they like to eat dead vegetation or dead insects. Should I step on it?

I knew that this was just a young creature, because I've read that in my part of the country the eggs usually hatch in May and the spider isn't

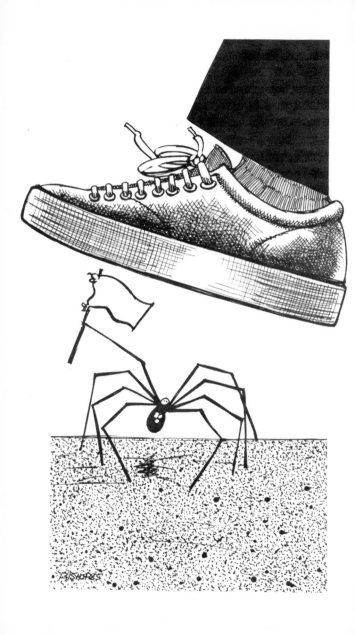

fully grown until July. How could I step on a baby daddy long-legs?

I knew that it wasn't going to make a web right there in the hospital, because daddy long-legs don't make webs. This little creature had probably hatched from an egg laid in the ground and should be living in protected places in a field or on an old log. Should I step on this little fellow, even though it might just have wandered in from a field and be looking for a way out?

I watched it as it slowly made its way across the floor, its body slung low between its eight long legs. I thought of how easily it could part with one of those legs, should another creature grab it. I also thought about those two little glands it has that give off a terrible odor, should any insect come too close. I could just about see its eyes looking out in opposite directions from a little mound on top of its head. I knew that all it could see in one direction was a big white tennis shoe. I wondered if it was preparing to part with a leg, or if it was making its terrible odor because of the threat that my tennis shoe posed. Should I lift my foot and smash it?

Then I thought of how helpless it really would be if I decided to step on it. I knew that God gave it those defenses—the eyes that look in opposite directions, the legs that come off easily, and the terrible odor—so that it could live well in its little world; but my world is too big for it.

God also gave me a "defense" so that I can live well—an ability to think. I get along fine in my world, but how would I feel if something much bigger than I decided to smash me, and I couldn't reason with him? Perhaps I should use my God-given "defense" to help this daddy long-legs which can't defend itself in my world. I didn't step on it.

I dried my hands, coaxed daddy long-legs onto a paper towel, and gently brought it outside. I think God smiled.

8

Pill Bug

It isn't a pill and it isn't a bug, yet we call it a pill bug. To most of us, any little thing that crawls is a bug. This little crawler, when disturbed, will curl up and look like a pill. Hence, the pill bug. Some people call it a wood louse. It's only one kind of wood louse; there are other kinds. None are really lice. Other people call it a sow bug. None of those names are very complimentary.

Unaware of the confusion surrounding its name, the little pill bug ambles through our lives more often than we know. And it does more good than we realize.

It's common under almost any rock or bit of rotting wood or bark on the soil surfaces, especially if there are plenty of dead leaves about. Many pill bugs living in one area have a great effect on the soil. They help break down leaf litter into smaller bits on which tiny soil-animals can feed.

You'll know a pill bug when you see it. Almost three-quarters of an inch long, it crawls about on seven pairs of legs. It has two long "feelers," or antennae, on the front of its head. Its oval body is covered by hard, smooth plates which fit together like an expansion watchband. If you poke it, it curls into its pill shape in defense.

Some wood lice that cannot curl up as completely as a pill bug have another defense. Special glands along the sides of their bodies ooze a sticky, nasty-smelling liquid. This may make a hungry spider change its mind about just how tasty a wood louse is.

Some wood lice feed only at night and stay out of the light. Pill bugs can venture out in the daytime, because their armor keeps them moist.

The pill bug's suit of armor may be just dandy protection, but it also causes problems. It's heavy and awkward, and it doesn't grow. When the pill bug grows too big for its skin, it must molt. After it wiggles out of its old skin it has a new, soft covering. The pill bug puffs up its body while the new skin hardens, so that there will be room to grow.

The little pill bug doesn't shed its whole skin at one time. That would leave it defenseless. Instead, it sheds only half at a time. The front half of the old skin comes off first. After it hardens and about two weeks pass, the back half comes off. If you find a pill bug, look at it closely. Usually it will be dark grey. But if one half is lighter than the other, it may be half molted.

A pill bug likes to live in moist places. The humidity should be 90 percent for the pill bug to be comfortable. In fact, this little bug has an amazing moisture sense. If you should put a pill bug in a dry container it will move around restlessly. Put a water-soaked cotton wad in the container, and the pill bug will scurry over to it and settle down.

Other moisture-loving creatures also have this sense. Scientists call it hygrokinesis, but the pill bug doesn't know that. It instinctively seeks out the place where it will live best.

The pill bug you find may look as if it's carrying a bulging pouch beneath it. This is a brood pouch, full of eggs. Pill bugs that hatch from these eggs look very much like their mother, but they are a little different. They are paler, and each has only six pairs of legs. When they molt for the first time they acquire their seventh pair.

During spring, summer, and fall, a pill bug scurries about the soil, feeding on dead plants. When the days grow cooler it crawls into a sheltering crack or cranny. It lies there quietly until spring comes and it can get back to work.

A pill bug and its wood lice relatives seem especially to prefer feeding on last year's wet leaf litter. The melting spring snows must uncover a real banquet for them—all those juicy, wet, rotten leaves!

That may not look appetizing to us, but I'm glad it does to a pill bug. After all, someone or something has to eat those leaves and help break them down. Else they'd pile up, and a forest would choke to death on its own litter. One naturalist has estimated that pill bugs and their relatives consume about one-third of the leaf litter in a forest. Other creatures with similar tastes take care of the rest.

You'll know a pill bug when you see it. It's the greyish "bug" that curls up into a "pill." Poke it once if you want to, and watch it curl. But let it stay where you find it. It has important work to do.

9

Black Widow

The name of this spider strikes fear into the hearts of many people. *Black widow*, that deadly spider! Stay away from the black widow!

I remember very well the first time I went walking in an area where black widows were known to live. I was petrified, sure that all the black widows out there were waiting just for me. I was certain that as soon as I stepped out the door, they would pounce, eager to do me in.

Why in the world would God create such a vicious little creature? Why did he make a spider that's so terribly dangerous to us?

The answer is: he didn't. Of course he made the black widow. But the black widow isn't a vicious little creature. That's just in our imaginations. And if we use our heads, the black widow isn't even very dangerous to us.

Yes, the black widow is poisonous. That's why we should use our heads when we deal with it. But its poison isn't as lethal as we imagine. Not everyone that's bitten by a black widow dies. In fact, only about four out of every one hundred black widow bites (to humans) are fatal. That counts only every hundred people who are *bitten*. That doesn't count the thousands of people who *see* black widows but are not bitten. Or the thousands more who pass a black widow web and never even see the spider.

But why must the black widow be that poisonous? Couldn't God have given it just a little bit of poison, maybe enough to kill an insect but not a person?

Perhaps we'll never know completely. One of the answers, I'm told, lies in the food that black widows eat. Like other spiders, they help keep the insect population in check. Apparently one type of insect they like is a big, hard, tough beetle. They need a potent poison to get through this beetle's tough outer shell. If just a little seeps in, it should be strong enough to kill the beetle quickly.

By the way, black widows do a lot of good from our point of view. Many of the insects they prey upon are serious crop pests. So they're really helping our crops.

Anyway, we know that God gave these spiders a powerful poison. He did that for a reason. But he did not create them to be vicious little creatures.

As far as spiders go black widows are really very timid. They would rather run than fight—fight humans, that is. A black widow is not looking for the first opportunity to bite you. It's looking for the first opportunity to get away from you. It will bite if it feels that you are threatening it. But then, what would you do if a creature thousands of times bigger than you poked you or threatened to squash you? You'd probably bite too. Don't bother a black widow and it won't bother you.

Besides making them naturally timid, God gave black widows all sorts of other characteristics that help us.

Black widows are web weavers. Usually they stick close to their homes. They don't wander all over the place as some spiders do. And because they're web weavers, their eyesight isn't particularly keen. You can see them long before they can see you. You are warned before they are.

Their webs are not particularly neat, as some spiders' webs are. They're an irregular mass of coarse, dark spider silk. Usually the spider rests on a silken sheet to one side of the web. So if you're in black widow area and you see an irregular web with a silken sheet next to it, you have a clue. You may be looking at a black widow's web.

Black widow's silk, by the way, is very interesting. Although it's coarse, as spider silk goes, it's much finer than the hair on your head. You would have to lay 5,000 strands of that silk side by

side to cover one inch. Yet it's very tough. It won't break or weaken even if it's boiled. You can handle it roughly and it won't break. Maybe it has to be tough to catch big, tough beetles.

A female black widow can spin up to 160 feet of silk a day. If you put all that silk into one long thread, that thread could reach from the top floor of a sixteen-story building down to the ground.

Most black widows spin their webs under bark or in other dark corners or crevices, usually near the ground. They live outdoors. You're not likely to find a black widow's web in the house.

Everybody knows what a black widow looks like, and that helps too. A female black widow is about one-half inch long, not particularly big as spiders go. She has a rounded black abdomen with red markings. Some females have a red hourglass shape on their undersides. Others have a series of red spots or red bars on the top of their backs. Black with these red markings means "watch out."

I used to wonder what good the red hourglass did on the female's *under*side. I'm not about to turn a spider over to find out if it's a black widow. This type of black widow, I discover, likes to hang on her web upside down. So you'll see the underside sooner than you'll see the upperside. The mark is in just the right place.

Male black widows are not as obvious as females. They're much smaller and they don't have the red marks. They just look like little normal black spiders. Why weren't they given warning markings? Because they usually don't bite. It's the female you must watch out for.

So there you have the black widow. It's a poisonous spider and you must be careful of it. But it's poisonous for a reason, and it's here for a reason. Besides that, God made it in such a way that we really don't have to be dreadfully afraid of it. He gave it a fear of humans, along with very distinctive markings. And he gave us brains to understand and appreciate his creation.

10

Tarantula

A few days ago our newspaper reported that tarantula sales are up. One local store sells between six and twelve of those big hairy spiders every week. People keep them as pets! Can you imagine that?

Maybe you *can* imagine that. Maybe you're one of those hardy (I'm tempted to say foolhardy) souls who own a tarantula. If so, you're a hardier soul than I. I could never keep a tarantula.

I realize that you probably keep that creature caged tightly in a terrarium. Even so, even with glass between me and it, I don't think that I could bring myself to look at it.

Tarantulas are so *big* for spiders. Their bodies can measure from one inch to almost three inches, front to back. And that's just the body. Then there are those big hairy legs. An average North American tarantula can measure about five inches when you include the legs. One South American variety has measured ten inches across, including the legs.

And they're so hairy! I know that the hair is there for a reason—defense. If a tarantula feels threatened, it works its hind legs rapidly over its hairy body and scrapes loose a small cloud of hair. That hair is almost like sneezing powder. It irritates eyes and noses. It's enough to chase away any small mammal. So if you ever see a tarantula with a bare patch on its body, you know that it has been in some tight scrapes lately. It's had to defend itself a bit.

Every time a tarantula molts (sheds its skin), it is provided with a brand-new set of hairs. So those hairs must be necessary. Some people think that tarantula hairs may contain poisonous substances. They say that if you preserve a dead tarantula in alcohol, even the alcohol with no hairs can sting. Something must leak from the hairs to the alcohol.

Most tarantulas are either a dark brown or black. One Mexican variety has reddish "knees." It really is quite pretty.

Did I say that? I suppose they all are OK. They're big and hairy, but I guess I could become used to that.

Some tarantula owners actually allow the spider to walk over them. They say that tarantulas are harmless, even a little shy. You wouldn't think that of such a big brute, but it's true. Most tarantulas are quite sluggish. They attack an enemy only when they're forced to do so. They'd much rather walk away than fight.

Before a tarantula attacks, it tries another defense. It rears up a bit on its hind legs, bringing its head up and showing those big fangs. That's usually enough to scare away anything. I know it would scare me away. Only if the "thing" keeps threatening does the tarantula bite.

Even then, its bite is not generally harmful to humans. We're too big, or its venom is too weak. We generally don't feel its effects.

The fangs, however, *can* pierce your skin. Some spiders are so small that they can't bite through human skin. Tarantulas are big enough to take a strong chomp and make it through the skin. I understand that it can hurt a bit, but it doesn't necessarily harm you.

Tarantulas are most likely to bite when you first acquire them as pets, the newspaper reported. That's because they're naturally shy and nervous. Wouldn't you bite, too, if a huge hand came after you? Apparently, if you treat them gently, they can become fine pets.

Perhaps . . . maybe . . . if I really screwed up my courage, I could let a tarantula walk over me. But I have no idea why I'd ever bother to do that. If you want to, go ahead. Apparently they're safe.

I think that I'd have problems feeding a pet tarantula. You actually have to open the cage and put the food inside. Apparently tarantulas in captivity eat a few crickets a week. You're supposed to throw the crickets in live, and follow with a dessert of a water-soaked sponge.

When they live free, tarantulas eat beetles, grasshoppers, and other insects and crawling creatures. They keep some of the bigger crawlers in check. Tarantulas in North America usually eat insects. The larger South American types sometimes prey on frogs, toads, mice, lizards, small snakes, and even small birds.

I suppose I could let the feeding go for a while. Some tarantulas in laboratories have lived for over two years without food and over two months without water. Yet, if I had a pet tarantula, I wouldn't want to be hard on it. I'd probably learn quite quickly to open the cage and throw in food.

One tarantula owner doesn't keep his spider in a terrarium. He lets the tarantula live on his living room curtains. Can you imagine that? Right out in the open on his curtains!

But then, most tarantulas that are free don't wander far. They dig little tunnels in the ground, cap them with a trapdoor, and hunt from there. They sit underneath the trapdoor and listen for prey to walk past. Then, pop-zap. They pop out of the trapdoor and zap their prey. At the most, a tarantula wanders about five feet from its burrow. I suppose that tarantula will stay on the curtain.

There's one exception. If that curtain-dwelling tarantula is a full-grown male, someone is in

Bishop 83

trouble. When the urge to mate hits this fellow, he'll range far and wide looking for a female. Usually this happens between August and October. So if you have a tarantula, keep it caged during that time. After it has mated, the male returns to his burrow.

The following summer the female lays about one thousand eggs. She spins a silken sheet, lays her eggs on the sheet, then covers them with another silken sheet. Then she crimps the edges of the two sheets together to form a loose bag. She watches over her eggs, as do many spiders. In fact, sometimes she hauls them out into the sunlight to warm them a bit. Six or seven weeks after the eggs are laid, they hatch. About one thousand small tarantulas leave the burrow.

If I ever bought a tarantula, I'd certainly make sure that it was not a female about to lay eggs. I'd hate to wake up some morning and find the terrarium crammed with one thousand tarantulas—even one thousand tiny tarantulas.

Not all those tiny tarantulas make it to adulthood. The young are often eaten by mice, birds, frogs, toads, lizards, and snakes. Come to think of it, that's just what some adult tarantulas eat. For a tiny tarantula's enemies, it sounds like a case of eat now or be eaten later.

I'm pretty sure that a tiny tarantula which escapes a mouse doesn't come back as an adult to eat that same mouse. That mouse is long dead by the time that tiny tarantula grows up. A tarantula must live for about ten years before it becomes an adult.

The male tarantula will be a real stay-at-home (or stay-on-curtains) until it becomes an adult. So if that person bought it when it was young, it may live contentedly on the curtains for a few more years.

Female tarantulas can live to a ripe old age of about twenty years. I suppose males could also. But their normal life span is a little over ten years. Apparently most of them lose their lives in the search for a mate.

Another time that tarantulas are in danger is when they molt. They do this four times a year during their first two years, then twice a year for the next three or four years, then about once a year until they become adults. Each time a tarantula molts, it comes out of its old shell with a soft new skin. That skin must dry and harden before it's good protection. While it's soft, the tarantula is an easy target. Usually it stays hidden in its burrow during this time.

I understand that the molting process is really something to watch. People with pet tarantulas have told me so. Pulling out of the old shell is quite a struggle and can take a while.

I almost watched the process once. Someone I know called and said that their tarantula was ready to molt. I was welcome to come and watch. So I went. While I was there, the spider just lay quietly, gathering strength for the big bust. That came after I left.

Come to think of it, I watched that tarantula and didn't feel creepy at all.

Maybe I could handle a tarantula pet. It might be rather interesting for a while. After all, tarantulas are good little creatures. They just happen to be very big spiders. They still are God's creatures, and he put them here for a good reason. They help keep little creepies in place.

On second thought, I think I'll treat tarantulas as I do all spiders. I'll leave them alone. They're fascinating and they're fine . . . right where they live.

11

Earwig on My Toothbrush

The only battle I ever waged with an earwig was really no contest. I won hands down—or rather, toothbrush down.

I first spied the critter sitting on my toothbrush—right on the bristles. (This was in the tropics, by the way. Critters on toothbrushes are common there.) I suspected, by the way it arched its little black body and waved those curved rear-end pincers at me, that this earwig was claiming my toothbrush as its own. Those pincers looked positively threatening, so I toyed with the idea of not brushing that day. But a sense of duty overcame my fear, and I really didn't want to give in to an inch-long "bug." So I gingerly picked up the very end of the handle as far away from the bristles as I could get. The earwig responded by arching higher and waving its pincers more. I could have sworn that the pincers grew and almost developed teeth, but that isn't possible. Anyway, the creature's whole bluff collapsed instantly when I merely flicked the toothbrush. The toothbrush dropped to the floor and the earwig scurried into a crack, obviously more afraid of me than I was of it. The last thing I saw were those rear-end pincers, untoothed and actually quite small. I imagine that the poor critter vowed never again to roam around after dawn.

I had probably caught it looking for one more snack before it turned in for the day. Earwigs move around at night, not during the day. That's why you don't see them often.

Besides that, they're black and flat. So if you're out at night when they're out, they're difficult to see. That's probably for their own protection.

Also, they like to crawl into cracks. They have a tendency to scuttle to a narrow place and squeeze in as soon as something touches them. Because they spend most of their time on soil (not on toothbrushes), they're constantly squeezing into cracks in the soil. Maybe that's why they were created so flat. So, unless you go around looking into soil cracks at night, you're not likely to see an earwig. Unless the earwig is confused, as this one must have been.

Maybe it mistook my toothbrush bristles for little plants. Earwigs eat a lot of plants. But usually they like decaying material or rotting plants. (That doesn't say much for my toothbrush.) Earwigs help break down these rotting plants so that any good minerals locked inside can be returned to the soil. Sometimes an earwig may catch a fly or two. Some rare earwigs even live on rats and bats. That's all good as far as most humans are concerned. An earwig on my toothbrush was not good, as far as I was concerned.

I must admit that, like most people, I was wary, if not downright afraid, of earwigs. Those black pincers can look absolutely dangerous. When it feels threatened, an earwig will arch its back to bring those pincers forward, as the one on my toothbrush did. You'd think twice before you did battle with those pincers. But most people in the know say those pincers can't pierce human skin. In other words, the earwig is more "bark" than "bite" as far as people are concerned.

As far as other earwigs are concerned, sometimes the "bark" comes with a "bite." Male earwigs do use those pincers to fight each other for desirable female earwigs. Sometimes the winner picks up the prize with his pincers and totes her to the nearest crack in the soil.

Believe it or not, female earwigs *can* be desirable. At least they're good mothers. Many insects "figure" that their duty is done once they lay eggs. But not Female Earwig. She lays 40 to 60 eggs (in the soil, of course) in either spring or fall and stays right there to guard them. When the eggs hatch, she actually feeds her tiny earwigs. She cares for them until they grow too big for

their skins and they molt. Then she decides, "That's enough." She crawls out of the soil, opens the nest, and 40 to 60 tiny earwigs scamper out to face the world.

I say "scamper" because most earwigs don't fly. Even the one on my toothbrush chose to hang on and take its chances rather than fly away. Earwigs have wings, but they don't use them often.

That's probably because earwig wings are so difficult to pack up and put away. The earwig's outer wings are usually short, leathery affairs. They're tough, and they're good protection for the inner wings. But the inner wings are larger than the covers. So, when an earwig folds its wings, it folds them from side to side and then from front to back. That's rather like one of us folding a big bed sheet to fit into a little pocket. So earwigs don't bother to fly that often. They'd rather walk.

Another thing that earwigs don't do is crawl into your ears. Their name suggests that they do, and lots of folktales would have you believe that, but it just isn't true. Everybody who knows earwigs says they don't like ears any better than any other "bug." What self-respecting insect would crawl into a human ear?

I must admit that I slept with the sheet over my ears for a few nights after our one-sided battle. I figured that if any earwig had cause to investigate an ear, it would have been *that* critter and *my* ear. But it didn't happen.

I assume the little loser crawled away with nary another thought about me or my toothbrush. I, the big winner, on the other hand, checked my sheets every night for at least a week. I never found an earwig waiting for revenge.

So it goes with earwigs and many other little critters. Somehow we make up tales about them. We know that they really won't crawl into our ears or sew our lips or bite off our toes, but we still wonder. Even full-grown people wonder just a little. We *know* that those pincers aren't going to deal us a death blow, but we still approach them with fear and trembling. I'll bet that if those little creatures knew how some of us big creatures tremble at their approach, they'd sit down and laugh. As it is, they just go about their business, as they were created to do.

The next time I see an earwig, I won't gear up for battle. I'll simply put it back in the soil where it belongs. Even if I find it on my toothbrush.

12

Noseeums

All things bright and beautiful,
All creatures great and small,
All things wise and wonderful,
The Lord God made them all.

That's what we sing, that's what we say, and that's what we believe—usually.

But noseeums just might be an exception to the rule. When a black cloud of these tiny critters flies right through your screen, you'd hardly call them bright and beautiful. They're certainly not great, as in "great big." In fact, they rate somewhere below "small." They're tiny—tiny pests. As they swarm around your legs and deliver their famous bites, I suspect that you'd be hard-pressed to call them wise or wonderful. You'd also probably be hard-pressed to admit that the Lord God made them all. Humanly speaking, it almost seems irreverent to "blame" noseeums on God.

You know what noseeums are, don't you? They're tiny, tiny insects that you don't see until you feel them. That's why people call them no-see-thems, or noseeums. They could just as well be named surefeelums; you can surely feel their bite.

Sometimes noseeums are called punkies. They're definite little insects; they're not just any little insect that bites. They're in the fly family. More accurately, they're called biting midges. More accurately yet, they're in the order *Diptera*, suborder *Nematocera*, family *Ceratopogonidae*. But even the scientific books, which give them names longer than their bodies, also call them noseeums.

If a noseeum measures one-tenth of an inch across from wingtip to wingtip, it's a big brute. Most measure a wingspread of one-twentieth of an inch. That's why they can fly right through your screens. Some other pesky fliers may be that small with their wings folded neatly at their sides, but they have trouble flying that way. No fly that I know of flies with its wings folded. So when other flies try to fly through your screens, their wings hit. But not noseeums. They cruise right on through those little squares with no trouble at all.

"Small" doesn't necessarily mean "simple"; neither does "tiny." Noseeums are flies; therefore they have all the fly parts. They may be miniature, but they are all there. They have one pair of wings and one pair of halteres (those knobby things that poke out of a fly's back, just behind its wings). Some noseeums have shiny wings. Could we call that bright? Others have hairs arranged in definite patterns on their wings. Someone has called that beautiful! (I have the book right in front of me to prove it.)

Noseeums also have six tiny legs and six tiny feet. Some have special feet—more about that later. They have two compound eyes, two antennae, and a mouth. What a mouth! I hate to say this, but only a female noseeum bites. She's the only one with the right equipment. Her mandibles (part of her mouth) look like little scissors blades. But she doesn't bother to cut neatly; she just puts them together and jabs—hard.

Noseeums also go through the complete fly life. A female lays eggs that hatch into wormlike larvae. These quiet down for a while to become pupae. That's when they change into full-blown adults, if you can call a noseeum full-blown.

Some noseeum larvae live in clear water. There they feed on things smaller than themselves. So, in their own little way, they help keep clear water clear.

In fact, although they're small, some larvae even reach out and grab their prey. They attach one silken thread to something solid—maybe a pebble—and let the current carry them. When they've gotten what they want, they follow their "lifeline" back home. That's almost wise.

Some noseeum larvae live in wet soil and de-

caying vegetable matter. They eat some of this decaying stuff and help break it down to smaller bits. Then creatures smaller than they are (there are such creatures) can use it and break it down

into even smaller bits. That's certainly necessary. It's almost wonderful.

So, noseeum larvae are helpful in their own small way. So are the adults. Sometimes noseeums swarm around flowers. They play an important part in the cross-pollination of spring flowers. Only the females do this. That makes up for the fact that only the females bite. Some noseeums prey on aphids, mealybugs, spider mites, spittle bugs, and bark beetles. So if noseeums swarm on you when you're in your garden, try to be glad that they're there. They're keeping your garden healthy. That *is* wonderful.

When female noseeums need blood (they need it to develop their eggs), they don't always look for us. Sometimes a caterpillar, a sawfly, or a frog will do just as well. How does that make you feel? Passed over for a caterpillar!

Some noseeums even prefer their close cousins, crane flies, and their very distant relatives, dragonflies. These noseeums have special feet that resemble little hooks. A noseeum can attach itself to the legs of another insect and hang on, like the "man on the flying trapeze," as the bigger bug glides through the air with the greatest of ease. These noseeums don't jam their scissors-like mouthparts boldly into the bigger bug's body. They delicately pierce one vein in one wing.

A few noseeums go for the wing veins of lacewings. These noseeums perch on a wing rather than on a leg because lacewings, which eat noseeums, can't reach them there. Some noseeums like blister beetle blood and oil beetle blood. Such little fellows really can't get through a beetle's tough shell. So they go for the tender skin *between* pieces of shell. And, believe it or not, some noseeums get their human blood secondhand. They actually chase a mosquito that has bitten a person and bite *it*. There seems to be some justice in that.

That's really a big list for such a little fly. It pollinates spring flowers and eats garden pests. It helps keep caterpillars, sawflies, frogs, crane flies, dragonflies, lacewings, blister beetles, and oil beetles in their places. And it even gets the last laugh on mosquitoes.

The last purpose alone—the bit about mosquitoes—is enough to keep me happy. I think I'd keep noseeums around just for that. They really do have a place.

All things bright and beautiful,
All creatures great and small,
All things wise and wonderful,
The Lord God made them all . . .
  even noseeums.

13

Fruit Flies for Dessert

"You'd probably find something good about this too," she said as she crushed the creature under her thumb. "She" was a dinner companion, sharing my table at a large banquet. "This" was a fruit fly.

"If the dessert is fruit, I'm not going to eat any," she announced loudly. "I don't want fruit flies for dessert." For emphasis she rolled her thumb once more over the tiny squashed fruit fly.

I wasn't in the mood for hailing forth on the virtues of fruit flies, so I covered my wince with a smile. There was a lull in the conversation. Had I been in the mood, I would have reminded her that we can thank fruit flies for much of the research that has been done in genetics. As a scientific tool alone, fruit flies have been priceless.

She probably wouldn't have been satisfied. She might have pointed out that we have *people* to thank for the research. Fruit flies have nothing to say about the matter. I could have answered her, I thought, with common sense.

Think for a minute about where you find fruit flies. Usually they collect near (as some books delicately state) "overripe" fruit. In other words, they like rotten fruit, right? What do you suppose they do with rotten fruit? They either eat it or lay their eggs in it. If they lay eggs in it, the hatching larvae probably eat the fruit.

The thought of flies or fly larvae eating your fruit probably isn't very appetizing to you. But the thought of your eating that rotten fruit isn't much better. At least the presence of fruit flies can warn you that your fruit is overripe.

Of course, a fruit fly's main goal in life isn't to tell you about the condition of the fruit in your fruit basket. That's only a sideline. Think about a fruit fly out in the open, away from all people and their fruit baskets. Where do you suppose you'd find it? Naturally, on rotting fruit!

Fruit flies, along with other little creatures, help clean the world of rotten fruit. Of course, one little fly can't perform the task alone. That's why, generally, the more rotten the fruit, the more numerous the fruit flies. Cleaning up rotten fruit may not sound like such an important job to you, but think about it. If all the wild berries, cherries, apples, and such were collected into one heap, you'd probably have a sizable mess. And something would have to clean it up. If you don't want the job, thank God for fruit flies and their kin.

I almost did tell my friend about the neat little body she had crushed under her thumb. But first I would have had to say everything you just read, so I kept silent.

I thought about how a fruit fly's mouth was created for sucking juices from rotten fruit. Its mouth looks more like a sponge-on-a-straw. The fly sets the bottom part, the "sponge," in a puddle of juice and sucks the juice up through a long tube-like "straw." Actually, a fruit fly drinks fruit juices.

I would have told her to look closely at those little red eyes. They're not single eyes. They're collections, hundreds and maybe thousands, of smaller facets. Each facet can see. Each fruit-fly eye is really many, many "eyes" put together. Besides that, I would have pointed out, those eyes are in a very good position for the fruit fly. The little creature can look ahead, downward, sideways, and upward all at the same time. It should be able to see where it's flying while it's looking for rotten fruit below and for danger from either side. Certainly a lot of care went into the design of those eyes.

I would have told her that even the hair of that little creature's body has a purpose. It helps the fruit fly sense humidity, temperature, and wind speed, all important information for such a little creature.

I almost told her about the fly's halteres. All flies have them; tiny fruit flies are no exception. Halteres are knobby little structures behind the fly's wings. I'm told that they are important for balance and flight control. Without them the fly can't maintain a straight course. Some flies can't even fly without their halteres. We don't have those little knobs figured out yet, but Someone does.

Someone also figured the right life cycle for a fruit fly. A female fruit fly will lay up to two

thousand tiny white eggs on decaying fruit. Because decaying fruit usually is quite soft and juicy, each of these eggs has a pair of "wings," or breathing tubes. These tubes extend beyond the juice to the air above, so none of the tiny eggs will drown in fruit juice. The larvae that hatch from the eggs live in the fermenting fruit. They survive—even thrive—in it.

The pupae (the cocoon-like stage of insect life) automatically move to the top of any juice puddle. They also have pairs of breathing tubes so that they won't drown. The adults, like the one my friend crushed, love rotten fruit.

I think my friend is one of those people who blame fruit flies for ruining fruit crops. I should have told her that that is not true. In fact, some people call the little fly she squashed a vinegar fly because it is attracted to the vinegar-like, yeasty odors of decaying fruit. That keeps it separate from flies like the notorious medfly, the Mediterranean fruit fly, which lays its eggs in developing fruit. The fly she crushed is from a family called *Drosophilidae*. The medfly and its kin are from a family called *Tephritidae*.

I almost told her that last bit of information, that what we usually call a fruit fly is not responsible for harming good fruit. But my thoughts were interrupted. At that moment a waiter passed our table. She grabbed his arm and told him that she didn't care for any dessert. "Too full," she fibbed.

I did say something then about everything having a place in creation, and everything being good in its place. "Yes," she agreed, "but not in my dessert." I said no more. But I smiled as the waiter brought ice cream for dessert.

14

Late September Serenade

In late September the serenade has begun. By night I hear crickets fiddling in the fields, telling the world that they are still looking for mates. By day I hear students fiddling in my classroom, telling the world that school has begun and that they haven't practiced much over the summer. This late September serenade is a unique combination of sounds.

Both kids and crickets started fiddling just a few weeks earlier. Most of my students played the previous year or have been playing for a few years. In a few weeks the sounds become music once again. Some have just started, but even their first sounds make sense to me.

The crickets are all beginners. Last year's

music-makers died with the first frost. These hatched from cricket eggs last spring. They didn't play earlier because they didn't have instruments. Only when they molted for the last time did they acquire their special file-and-scraper wings. And then only the males were given noise-makers. The female crickets' lot in life is to sit and listen to the males fiddle.

I feel a close kinship to female crickets at that time of the year. It's my lot in life also to sit then and listen to a group of beginners fiddle for the first time. Only another music teacher can understand the absolute joy I feel when I hear a recognizable form of "Twinkle, Twinkle, Little Star" for the first time. Usually I recognize it long before anyone else does. My ears have become tuned to that sound.

So, too, the female cricket. Her ears—which are on her front knees—are tuned to the song of a male just like her. Different kinds of crickets sing different songs. Some chirp more times per second than others. To us the sounds simply say, "We're a bunch of crickets in a field." Ms. Cricket hears, "I'm not your kind." "Neither am I." "I am. Come over here." Somehow, in the din, she can pick out the sound that is special music to her ears—sort of the way I can hear "Twinkle, Twinkle" when no one else can.

I must make one point in defense of my struggling young charges. This weather wreaks havoc with stringed instruments. Warm, humid days and cool nights pop strings and throw instruments out of tune. Pegs stick and bows won't behave, so the quality of the "music" suffers. But I take that all into account and can still make sense of the sounds.

Crickets, of course, don't have that problem. The files and scrapers they carry on their wings never need restringing or repair. Yet their song does change with the weather. As the temperature rises, they chirp faster. But Ms. Cricket takes that into account. As the male warms up and chirps faster, she warms up and responds to the faster chirps.

A male cricket usually digs a burrow or finds a little sheltered place he can call home. He'll even fight other crickets for his choice piece of turf.

After he has eaten his fill of just about anything that might be edible, he sits at his doorway and grooms himself. He runs his antennae through his jaws, sticks his feet in his mouth to bite off dirt, and carefully scrapes his belly on the ground. Then he dusts his instrument—he swings his wings forward and scrapes off every bit of dirt.

As the sun sets, he sits on his front porch and sings. The female cricket, lured by his song, comes hopping right up to his front door.

I wish that my students would keep their instruments as clean and conditioned. Every year I go through my little song and dance of "How to Care for Your Instrument." Yet bows break, instruments gather rosin dust, and strings acquire knots "all by themselves." But then, these kids are hardly ever rewarded by the sight of people crowding to the door at the first strains of "Twinkle, Twinkle."

Of course, we make our music for different purposes. Those crickets sing so loudly in the fields because they're advertising for mates. They're not "thinking" of much else. I suppose that's not the most noble of purposes, but that's the way they were created. Yet they sing and they hear just right, automatically, without hours of practice. And in so doing, their songs are a testimony to the wisdom of their Creator.

I tend to lose sight of my purpose during this September din. Sometimes I have to remind myself that I chose to do this because I think that music is such a wonderful means of praise. If I can give some of my students this means of praising their Maker, it's worth the effort. I'll fix strings, train little fingers, and listen with all my heart for the first strains of "Twinkle, Twinkle."

We may not sound like much to you right now, but we're trying. And I'm sure that, as we fiddle by day and the crickets fiddle by night, the Creator can sort out all those sounds. It may sound like noise to a casual listener, but to his ears I'm sure it sounds like a beautiful late September serenade.

15

Blue Racer

"Come outside. There's a *huge* snake on the path!"

With that call to arms I rushed outside, fully prepared to demonstrate my fearless nature. I grabbed a big stick on the way down the path. I wouldn't kill the snake, I decided bigheartedly. I'd simply chase it off the path to clear the way for people more fearful than I. If it were huge, it might fight for its right in the sun, but *I* would show it who was boss. I would stand my ground until the snake slithered away in defeat.

Nearing the spot, I crawled up on a log, my stick ready to beat back any fierce fangs. No sense in taking any chances, I figured.

There it lay, five feet ahead of me, sprawled out

in a sunny spot on the path. It hadn't noticed me yet, so I had time to consider this fearsome creature with which I would soon do battle.

Its upper parts were colored a deep blue-black, while its chin and throat showed a creamy white. Parts of its belly that showed were colored that same creamy white.

"Blue racer!" I thought, and my heart beat a little faster. Racers are at home in trees and bushes as well as on the ground. That snake could crawl up onto my perch if it wanted to. Some snakes can't.

Had I been standing poised on a log in another part of the country I might have thought black racer, brown-chinned racer, tan racer, or one of eleven names. Blue racers are common in Michigan; other racers live in other parts of North America. Basically they're all the same type of snake, just colored differently.

Racers and several other snakes (including the coachwhips) all belong to the same family. The scientific name of that family is *Colubridae*; usually it's called the "typical-harmless-snakes" family.

"But you never know," I thought as I shifted my weight on that log. "Some snakes in the family have venom and are dangerous to people." (Three types are, but they live in Africa.)

"Besides," I argued with myself, "This snake is huge. It's at least *three* feet long." I mentally laid it alongside a yardstick. "Almost three feet." I checked to be sure that I was no closer than five feet.

Actually, the average length for a blue racer is about four feet. Sometimes racers grow to be over six feet long. But this three-footer was long enough for me.

I couldn't tell if it was male or female. A male racer's tail is usually longer and thicker at the base than a female's tail. Frankly, I couldn't tell where the body ended and the tail began.

"Probably it will put up a good fight," I thought grimly. "This certainly is an adult. It has fought before." Young racers hatch between July and September. When they hatch, they're only eight to thirteen inches long. This was only July, and since this snake was so big, it definitely had not hatched recently. It was at least a year old. Besides, young racers are colored differently from this snake. They have spots and blotches on their sides and back. They take two to three years to mature.

I really wasn't sure about my fear that this snake would put up a good fight simply because it was an adult. Snakes hatch with all their instincts intact. No parent snake lingers to teach its babies how to fight. Baby snakes know already. Age has nothing to do with it.

"Yet this one might have learned something," I thought as I shifted the stick in my hand.

Suddenly the blue racer saw me!

As long as I hadn't moved, I was a tree as far as that snake was concerned. But I had moved. Snake eyes were created to see movement, not still-standing objects. It turned its head a bit sideways to see me better. Snakes have good side vision, but they don't see things directly ahead very well.

I stared into its unblinking eye, trying to make it blink or look away. However, snakes can't blink.

They don't have eyelids. Instead, they have transparent scales that always cover the eyes to protect them. A yellowish lens covered this racer's eye. Although many snakes are night-active, a racer is day-active. Since it cannot blink or squint, the colored lens protects its eye from too much sun-

light. Still the snake stared at me. I finally blinked and looked away.

"Time for action," I thought. Slowly I dangled one foot from the log. Instantly blue racer reacted. Its long forked tongue flicked in and out of its closed mouth.

Snakes are one of the few creatures that can stick their tongues out without opening their mouths. Each snake has a little notch in its lower jaw especially for that.

That tongue, I knew, was chemically sensing my presence. Inside a snake's head, on its upper jaw, lie two small openings to two passages. These passages are packed with sensitive cells. When a snake flicks its tongue out, it gathers "odor molecules" floating in the air. When the tongue flicks into the mouth, each fork goes into an opening. The molecules travel up the passages, and the sensitive cells tell the snake what it is smelling.

I knew that blue racer couldn't bite me with that tongue. Tongues don't bite. But I didn't like it smelling me that way.

"Go away," I commanded loudly. "Scram."

The blue racer didn't move. Snakes are deaf to sounds that we hear. They have no outer ears. But they are very sensitive to vibrations carried through the ground. That's the way they hear.

"Time to close the gap and do battle," I thought, still perched on my log. Suddenly all the descriptions I had read about racers flashed through my mind.

AGGRESSIVE. Actually, the complete description would read "aggressive toward small mammals." But right then I considered myself a small mammal.

ACTIVE AT 70° F TO 86° F. Snakes are cold-blooded; their bodies take the temperature of the air about them. When the temperature falls below 70° F, a racer must rest. It's too cool to move quickly. When the temperature falls below 40° F, a racer must hibernate. It was 80° F that day. The blue racer was active.

AGILE, GRACEFUL. The blue racer has no problem slithering over the ground or up trees—or logs. In fact, it does move gracefully.

FAST-MOVING. Fast for a snake, that is. The fastest snake in North America covers ground at a record-breaking pace of five miles an hour. Almost any person can run faster than that.

I lowered to my foot and stamped the ground. The blue racer shifted nervously. Then it *rattled*!

I froze. What was that? Did I have a strange-looking rattler instead of a harmless blue racer? Then I remembered. When a blue racer feels threatened or annoyed, it makes a rattling noise by vibrating its tail tip in dead vegetation.

Determined not to be frightened by this bluff, I moved two steps toward the blue racer. It slithered two steps away. I took two bigger steps. It slithered five steps away. Two more steps took me to the spot where it had first rested. The blue racer disappeared. The battle was over. It never really began.

I dropped my stick and walked back to the cabin. "What a shame," I thought. "I should have had my camera. Blue racer really was a beautiful little snake."

Blue racer was a typical snake. Most snakes fear people. In fact, they're more afraid of people than people are of them.

16

Harry's Cobra

Harry, one of my friends in Borneo, used to joke about the cobra that lived under his house. Now, the fact that it lived under his house doesn't mean that it could do no harm. Houses there are on stilts; you go down to go out. "Under" is ground level.

Harry used to tell us that he'd whistle the Canadian national anthem (Harry is Canadian) to warn his cobra that he was coming down. At night, he said, he'd whistle the anthem *and* turn on all the lights.

I think that a lot of what Harry said was designed to impress young females new to the tropics. It did. We always wore sturdy shoes and made a lot of noise when we walked over to Harry's house.

Maybe Harry was telling us, in his own way, to walk carefully. Cobras are all over Borneo, as they are all over southern Asia, India, and Africa. Their bite is deadly. About 30,000 people die in Asia each year from snakebite, most of them from cobra bite. Maybe Harry just wanted to be sure that the number didn't rise to 30,002.

Actually, cobras are quite sluggish as far as snakes go. And they're quite shy; even the Canadian national anthem will scare them away. But because they're rodent eaters they often live near villages, where rats and mice abound. When cobras rest in long grass, they're pretty well hidden (hence the phrase "snake in the grass"). Villagers tend to walk barefooted. A bare foot on an unsuspecting cobra invites disaster. That's why we wore sturdy shoes to Harry's house.

Actually, Harry seemed to like his cobra. He said that it kept the mice and rats away. He was probably right. I think that's why cobras are there.

I also think that's probably why cobras have such powerful venom. Rats are big there. (The first time I saw one, honest-to-goodness, I thought I was looking at a gopher about the size of a squirrel.) Cobra venom can subdue a big rat and actually cause a relatively painless death within minutes. That's a little easier on the rats, and fewer rats are a lot better for people, as long as people are careful of the cobras. I was always careful of Harry's cobra.

Harry's cobra was probably a regular Asian

cobra (*Naja naja*), which eats rats and mice and gathers near villages. Asian cobras are quite small as far as tropical snakes go. Harry claimed that his was six feet long. Usually they're only about four or five feet long. Maybe Harry exaggerated a little.

Yet a cobra does appear rather ferocious when you first see it. If it has seen you first, it's generally reared up, the front part of its body standing straight up from the ground. And its hood is out. It can puff out its neck extra wide, just below its head. That's the cobra's way of warning you that it's bothered or afraid. It will strike if you continue doing whatever it is you're doing. Actually, I think that's rather sporting of the snake. It warns before it does anything drastic. All you have to do is stay alert when you are in cobra country.

Once Harry tried to claim that his was probably a king cobra (*Ophiophagus hannah*). We knew better than to accept that. King cobras can grow to a length of about eighteen feet, not a puny six. Besides, they eat other snakes, not rats and mice. So they usually live in the jungle, not near villages.

King cobras carry enough venom to kill several people with one bite. Yet they don't often do that. Because king cobras live in the jungle, they don't have much contact with people. Besides, an eighteen-foot, twenty-pound snake is fairly easy to see, even in the jungle. People don't step on king cobras by mistake.

All cobras, by the way, can open their mouths

only so wide—wide enough to get a big rat. That's not wide enough to bite a person on any part of the body except on a leg or an arm. Snake charmers in India know this and keep their arms and legs close to their bodies, out of reach.

One type of African cobra, the spitting cobra (*Naja nigricollis*), doesn't bite for defense. It bites only what it eats. It spits for defense. It can spray twin jets of venom a distance of eight feet. Usually it aims for an enemy's eyes. They say this venom stings fiercely and can cause blindness. It doesn't cause death.

The way this cobra's fangs are made is interesting. Other cobras' fangs have holes in the bottom. When the snake bites, the venom drips out of these holes. The spitting cobra, however, has holes in the front center of its fangs. These holes are very small, producing a nozzle effect. The cobra just looks at the intruder and spits out through the front of its teeth.

Why in the world does this cobra spit, when others bite? It lives in an area where antelope and other hoofed animals graze. An antelope hoof is rather tough to bite, even for a cobra. An eight-foot jet spray aimed at an animal's eyes, however, gives that animal ample warning that it is about to step on a cobra.

So you see, even cobras have been given just what they need for their lifestyle. There's a purpose for their presence, and that purpose is good. We must simply treat them with the respect they deserve, and never surprise them.

We never surprised Harry's cobra. In fact, we never *saw* Harry's cobra. Sometimes I wonder if it was really there.

17

A Lizard in My Honda

I've never seen a frilled lizard. I did see a news clip about one last week, however. In the film the lizard was ambling about, acting very lizard-like. When the camera moved in, the lizard sat up and took notice. It looked straight at the camera, opened its mouth, and hissed. Suddenly a huge flap of skin around its neck ruffled up as if someone had blown air into it. Bright spots of black, brown, red, yellow, and white glowed on this huge frill. The lizard leaned closer and opened its mouth wider. I could see its teeth and the bright red interior of its mouth. It hissed again and swayed threateningly toward the camera.

Had I been behind that camera, I would have dropped my equipment and run. This photographer persisted.

Suddenly the lizard did an about-face. It dropped on all four legs and ran. But it wasn't about to disappear without a show. About three feet down the path it reared up on its hind legs . . . and kept running! With its front legs pumping the air, it looked for all the world like a miniature jogger with a big ruffled collar—except that its tail flew straight out behind it.

About ten feet down the path it stopped and looked over its shoulder. Sighting the camera, it turned and literally hightailed it out of there on two legs.

My attention captured, I watched the rest of the news clip. I was really hoping to catch one more glimpse of this comical creature. But the news person continued: This lizard has captured the hearts of the Japanese. A TV film brought it stardom. Now it's the main attraction of Saturday morning cartoons in Japan. And its inflatable plastic look-alike, a toy, is selling faster than it can be made. This whole frilled lizard craze, the news reported, began when the creature was used in a car commercial on Japanese television.

I drive a Honda, made in Japan. So when I heard that last bit of news, my imagination began to run about as fast as that frilled lizard had in the news clip. I pictured several car commercials, all of which included the lizard in my Honda.

Before I tell you about those, however, you should understand that the scene the lizard made was in self-defense. Although the news clip didn't say so, that's the way God enables it to protect itself. First it bluffs when danger threatens. It pretends to be big and vicious. If that doesn't work, it runs for its life. All the time the lizard is really frightened.

Now, for the first commercial, I imagined my green Honda on a car lot. No one is nearby except the lizard, who's looking over the car. A salesperson comes up and the lizard shifts nervously.

"How much for this Honda?" it hisses, worried about the price.

"That little beauty? Only _____ yen," answers the salesperson.

"That much?" The lizard's mouth drops open and its frill rises. Maybe it can bluff the salesperson into lowering the price.

"Not a yen less," comes the firm reply.

With that the lizard runs—"Get me out of here!" "Are you sure?" it calls over its shoulder. And it disappears around the corner to another car lot.

However, that may not have been the scene at all. Perhaps the car dealer wanted to point out how comfortable the car is. Picture the lizard inside my Honda, driving through Tokyo. "Warm in the winter, cool in the summer," the ad says. "A heater and an air-conditioner (don't I wish) that are designed to please even a lizard."

That would be quite a claim. You see, a lizard is coldblooded. Its body takes the temperature of the air around it. On cold days it must sit in the sun to warm itself through and through. On

warm days it must seek shade; it cannot perspire to cool itself. Most lizards naturally seek sun and shade at the right times. I suppose, though, that maybe some strange, unnatural lizard would like a heated, air-conditioned car.

A lizard's blood circulation differs from ours because its heart differs. It usually has less oxygen in its body. After it runs or is very active, it must rest a long time to replenish its oxygen. That's why lizards spend quite a bit of time sitting absolutely still, resting.

That bit of information brought this next ad to my mind: the frilled lizard and my Honda race down a path. Lizard stops soon to rest. Honda keeps going. "This car never needs to rest," the announcer says. "Because of a unique air-flow design, it can run for hours."

Or maybe they were advertising the size of my Honda. They could put the lizard next to a Komodo dragon and say, "Some are too big." Then they could put the lizard next to a gecko and say, "Some are too small." Finally they would put the lizard in my Honda and say, "Some are just right."

At three feet from head to tail, the frilled lizard

measures a resounding "average" for lizards. The Komodo dragon, a lizard which lives on a few tropical islands, grows to ten feet in length. Some gecko lizards are only one and one-half inches long.

Or perhaps they were trying to show my Honda's good points. They might zoom in on the lizard's four feet, then take a closeup of the four claws on each foot. "It grips the road to get you going," the announcer drones. Next they pan the scaly body. "It's tough and durable, in forest or desert, wet weather or dry," he continues. Then they take a closeup of the eyes. The lizard blinks, so everyone can see the eyelid with its protective scales. "Efficient and protective, it allows you excellent vision in rainshowers or sandstorms," he adds.

Finally the camera backs off to show the whole lizard in my Honda, catching and eating insects, as all lizards do. "You can be sure that there are no 'bugs' in this car," he finishes.

I really don't know how they used a frilled lizard to advertise a car, but it was fun to imagine. I imagine that the advertisement was probably a little farfetched.

A frilled lizard, I would think, is not a very good advertisement for a car. It is, however, an excellent advertisement for its Creator.

18

Gerbils

Often when we talk about creation and how wonderfully God made everything, we mention things "out there." We agree that animals such as camels, elephants, or even porcupines have their place in creation, but most of us don't have much experience with them. Even little creatures that we may know, such as spiders and grasshoppers, are wonderfully made for their lives, but we really see little of them. They scramble or scurry past us "out there," but not many of us have a chance to sit down and watch them.

I'd like to tell you about an animal that most people know. You may have had one as a pet or seen one in your classroom. Almost everyone has had a chance to handle gerbils. But their familiarity doesn't make them less interesting.

The type of gerbil that people keep as pets is not native to North America. It lives naturally in the Gobi Desert regions of Mongolia in eastern Asia. It happens to be a curious, pleasant, gentle animal that doesn't seem to mind becoming a family pet. That's probably why it's so popular. But if you look at your gerbil closely, you'll see how wonderfully it was created for desert living.

Gerbils are covered with fur from the tips of their noses to the tips of their tails. Fur even covers the soles of their feet. This fur insulates them from the desert heat. Gerbils scampering across hot sand never burn their feet because they have fur "hot pads" to walk on.

Why do you think gerbils have fur on their tails? That's convenient in a desert. Gerbils often sit on their hind legs and use their tails as props. So the tails are insulated; they, like the feet, won't burn in the sand.

Even the gerbils' color protects them. It's a tweedy, tawny brown. If it were pure white or black, it would contrast sharply with bare, sandy soil. A hawk or other enemy could easily spot black or white gerbils. But because they're the same color as their desert home, they can scamper about unnoticed.

Gerbils' ears are large for their little bodies. They're also well-developed, designed to pick up the faintest desert sounds.

Their hind legs are bigger and stronger than their front legs. This makes it easy for gerbils to hop, and hopping is the best way to move on hot sand. Besides that, hopping is a good way to escape enemies. Gerbils can leap in any direction—forward, backward, sideways, or straight up in the air. They can even zigzag or turn in midair.

The insides of gerbils' bodies, like the outsides, are wonderfully adapted to desert life. Although they will drink available water, gerbils can get along quite well without any. They receive all the moisture they need from seeds and grains. Fats are changed within their bodies to give them the water and energy they need.

When gerbils have no drinking water, their blood becomes a little thicker than usual. But it never becomes too thick to flow freely through their bodies.

Gerbils' kidneys are especially efficient. They take almost every bit of precious water from wastes, so the little animals lose only a few drops a day. Food wastes, too, are concentrated automatically, so that no moisture is lost.

Gerbils can live in temperatures as high as 110°F for up to five hours. They can also survive temperatures as low as 0°F. That's good in the desert because, while days are blazing hot, nights are often freezing cold.

Gerbils are usually active both day and night. They do tend to stay in their burrows through the hottest part of the day and the coldest part of the night.

Their underground burrows are usually sev-

eral feet long, with branch tunnels at different levels and chambers used for nesting and food storage. There are several entrances to these burrows, but the gerbils often plug and unplug them. This helps confuse their enemies. It also helps keep moisture and an even temperature inside the burrow.

Gerbils will live in colonies, but males often mark their own territories within the colony. They have special scent glands on the undersides of their bellies, which they rub on stones and other objects.

Female gerbils have scent glands too, but they use these glands to mark their babies. Then they know which young gerbils are their own.

Male and female gerbils tend to mate for life. Usually they'll have their first litter when they're about fifteen weeks old. The female is ready to mate again right after she has had a litter. But if she's nursing a large litter of little gerbils, an unusual thing happens. The babies developing inside her body stop growing and just wait. When the nursing gerbils begin to eat solid food, the developing babies pick up where they left off. They finish developing and are born a few weeks later.

This is all very interesting for gerbils living in the Gobi Desert. It's also necessary to know if you want to have gerbils living at your house. It's usually wise to buy two males or two females from the same litter. They'll live together peacefully and won't produce a litter every few months.

Gerbils usually stop producing litters when they're about one and a half years old, but they can live for up to five years. So a pair of older gerbils may also make good pets.

Most of what I told you is about gerbils living free in the desert. But that's still "out there." What about your pet gerbils? They're the same animals. You can see in your pet gerbils all the special features God gave them for living in the desert, because that's where they were created to live.

Some wild animals must live free. That's why people don't often keep pet woodchucks or wolverines. But gerbils are basically pleasant, adaptable little creatures. They tend to regard their cages as home. Even if you do let them run free, they like to eat and sleep in familiar surroundings. That's what makes them such good pets.

So if you have gerbils or know someone who does, you can have a good time with them. Look closely at them and think about where they live naturally. The wonders of creation aren't always "out there." They're as close as you care to look.

19

Chippy

Oh, how I wanted to see a deer! I would really like to have seen three or four together. If I had my way, they'd be standing right in front of our cabin early some morning. But I'd settle for one deer or maybe even just a white tail disappearing into our woods. Couldn't I at least see a deer track?

We had owned the little piece of woods for over a year already, and I hadn't seen much of any wildlife. At least Wayne had one badger to his credit, but I had seen nothing bigger than a chipmunk. Whenever someone would ask me what wildlife I had seen up there, I'd mutter, "Only a chipmunk," and change the subject. I was downright embarrassed.

Chippy didn't seem to be the least embarrassed about being "only a chipmunk." In fact, I think he rather enjoyed it.

Weighing in at less than half a pound and measuring only about nine inches (a lot of which is tail) from stem to stern, cheerful Chippy can't make his way in the woods by brute force. He doesn't have enough of it. But he certainly has lots of other things going for him.

Colored a rusty brown with telltale stripes down his back and on his face, Chippy blends well with his usual background of dried leaves and dappled sunlight. If he chooses to freeze in his tracks, he's almost invisible on the forest floor.

Chippy sports two handy stretchable pockets inside his cheeks. They extend from his jawbone well down his neck and serve perfectly as shopping bags when he starts stowing away nuts for the winter. It would take him an awfully long time to stash away one-half to one bushel of nuts and grains if he had to carry them home bit by bit. His pockets help him cut his work time to manageable hours.

Chippy has typical rodent teeth. His four front incisors—two on top and two on bottom—grow continuously. Enamel on the back of his teeth is thinner than enamel on the front, so the back wears away faster. This keeps a good cutting edge on Chippy's teeth. He can chisel through a hickory shell any time he pleases.

Chippy's short front legs are very strong, so he can dig easily. That's a big help, since he digs his home.

Of course, Chippy burrows out his underground home by instinct; he doesn't think about it. But that burrow is still designed to help him survive in the woods. The entrance tunnel is only about two inches wide—wide enough for Chippy, but not much else. His actual den is usually about five feet below ground level, below the reaches of frost and flood. Several tunnels usually lead off the main den. These tunnels are loosely plugged with dirt to keep out uninvited guests while providing emergency escapes. Whenever he builds an entrance tunnel, Chippy will scatter the dirt he's dug up so that no telltale mound remains at his door.

Chippy's burrow is so well-planned, in fact, that it often stays very cool on hot summer days, very warm on cool autumn days, and very safe year 'round.

Chippy doesn't hibernate completely during the winter. He does sleep very deeply (his pulse rate and temperature drop), but he wakes up once in a while, sometimes just to grab a bite to eat.

In the summer Chippy likes to eat mushrooms, berries, snails, earthworms, millipedes, insects, nuts, and seeds. He likes berries, seeds, and nuts best. When he does his fall shelf-stocking, he instinctively eliminates anything damp, like mushrooms and berries. Those foods might rot in his burrow. Instead he takes only dried food; so his winter fare is likely to be mostly nuts and dried seeds.

Chippy doesn't mind the company of humans too much. He or one of his friends—I can't tell them apart—would chatter at us when we first arrived, but he'd soon settle down and go about his business.

His business soon became our business. Because Chippy was the only animal bold enough to show himself, we began feeding him—sort of.

I took two pounds of peanuts up especially for him. He soon learned to come right to the door for his nuts. But chipmunks take longer to eat peanuts than people do. We found we were eating most of them in our efforts to tame Chippy.

Just about the time I was running out of peanuts, Chippy was running out of caution. Early one morning we heard him *inside* the cabin. He was running around between the ceiling and the roof. I first thought it was a rat, but he had left peanut shells all over the place, so we knew who it was.

We surely hadn't planned on that. We had invited him *up to* the cabin, not *inside*. Time to stop the peanuts.

Poor Chippy probably wondered. After all, we had encouraged him.

Later in the summer we put birdfeeders out and loaded them with seeds. Who was first to help himself? Chippy, of course. Wayne became rather upset. He'd sit on the porch for hours and yell whenever Chippy dared to go near a feeder. But we couldn't change Chippy's ways.

Finally we greased one feeder pole. Poor

Chippy took one flying leap at it, landed on the ground with a thud, and never tried again.

The other feeder was on a high, fat stump—much too large for grease. So we wrapped tinfoil around the stump. This stumped Chippy, but just for a little while. He tried it once, then just sat looking at it. Then he kept running up it until he had clawed the foil to tatters. A few hours after we had put the foil up, Chippy was sitting in the feeder again. I think he winked at me.

I found myself almost becoming angry with Chippy. Those seeds weren't for him, they were for the birds.

Poor Chippy probably couldn't figure us out at all. We put food right in the middle of his territory and then chased him away from it. That's sort of like someone putting a nice juicy hamburger on your supper plate and then slapping your hands every time you pick it up.

We finally reached an uneasy truce with Chippy. We didn't chase him from the feeder, but he also got a lot of his food from the woods.

By November, Chippy's sleeping most days. Birds still come to the feeders. Some don't mind having us around; others fly away as soon as we move.

We have seen deer tracks, by the way, right past the bedroom window and down our driveway. We haven't seen the deer. They come and go while we're sleeping, I suspect.

I suppose I won't see a deer. They're too wary; that's their way. And I suppose Chippy and I will argue again next summer. He's bold; that's his way. I did learn a lot about those animals last summer. I especially learned that I can't force them to act the way I want them to act. They follow their instincts; that's their way. And that's best.

20

Meet Pat

Meet Pat, but don't try to pet, or even pat, Pat.
Don't even try to shake Pat's paw. She just may
turn her back on you. You'll have her tail instead,
and a porcupine's tail is not a very pleasant thing
to shake. Neither is her back or her head, for that
matter. Only her nose and belly are free of those
long quills, and whoever heard of shaking noses
or bellies? Unless you want a painful introduc-
tion, forget the niceties when you meet Pat the
porcupine.

Pat has a habit that you may as well know
about right away, so that you're not offended. She
never meets a dangerous situation head on; she'd
rather meet it tail on. If she considers you a
dangerous situation, you'll know it when she

turns her back on you.

Her quills are also a pretty good indication of her state of mind. If she leaves them tucked beneath her longish brown fur, you don't have to worry, because she's not worried. If they're sticking straight out in the air, like pins stuck the wrong way into a pincushion, worry. She's got a bunch of extra-thick quills on her back and her tail. One swipe of her tail could get you into a very painful situation.

Pat is generous to a fault with her quills. If you give her any trouble, she'll give you some quills. That's trouble for you, so she figures that it's an even exchange. The quills are rather easy to get; they're just hard to get out. Each quill bears its own special gift—little barbs that point the wrong way. They allow the quill to go into your hand or leg, or wherever, very easily. But when you try to pull the quill out, the little barbs stick tightly in your flesh. Pat's gift is one you can't get rid of very easily.

Pat can. She doesn't throw her quills, as some people accuse her of doing. She merely brushes or slaps you with them. They're very loosely connected to her, but they can become very tightly connected to you.

Pat's quills are hollow inside. That doesn't make them hurt less, it just makes them lighter for her to carry around. Four thousand of them weigh one ounce. Pat's thirty thousand quills add only seven and one half ounces to her weight. Each quill is about three inches long, so she's got a lot of trapped air floating around her.

Because of all the air she carries with her, Pat's not afraid of water. She bobs on it like a beach ball. She couldn't possibly sink, and she knows it. But she doesn't swim very often; she prefers to waddle through the forest.

She really does waddle most of the time. There's nothing skinny about Pat. You could honestly call her "fat Pat." Even when her quills are down, she looks like a brown wad of waddling fur. She's only three feet long, but she weighs between fifteen and twenty pounds.

During cold weather she wears her thick winter underwear. It does nothing for her appearance, but it does keep her warm. She chooses a style that looks like brown sheep's wool and fits snugly under her regular fur. It falls out in the spring. Then she looks a little more sleek. Still, coming or going, Pat looks just plain fat.

If you get a chance to see her coming, take a peek at those bright orange teeth. They look as if she's never brushed them. She probably hasn't, but she does sharpen them regularly. Like all rodent teeth, they'll grow forever if given the chance. Pat doesn't give them the chance. She files them down on hard plants and on tree bark.

Her quill-less nose is a sharpie. She can smell if something is friend or foe. She can smell if something is food or feeder. She can even smell if her food has been salted.

Her quill-covered ears are sharpies too. She can hear animals tromping through the forest long before she can see them.

Her eyes are so poor that she can hardly see. If she waddles into something that isn't moving, she doesn't even bother to try to see it. She'll smell it instead. If something moves, she may try to see it. Usually, by the time she's lumbered up to it, it's moved away.

She's got whiskers on the side of her face. They're not very ladylike, but they are porcupine-like. They're Pat's sense of touch. By scraping her whiskers between two branches, she can tell if there's room enough for the rest of her to squeeze through. You won't often find Pat help-lessly wedged into places where she shouldn't be.

Since her sense of touch grows out of her face, her paws are free for climbing. She's got long, sharp front claws that she can stick into a tree like grappling hooks. She gives her fat body a boost with her tail and then sinks in her sharp claws higher up the tree. She climbs up head-first, just as you'd expect. She climbs down tail first, using her tail to tell her when she's hit bottom. She couldn't see it, anyway, with her poor eyes.

Maybe it's a good thing that Pat can't see very well. She might become scared if she ever met another porcupine. She can smell one, but she doesn't know that her kind is really not a sight for sore eyes. You see, lots of animals groom their fur, but Pat doesn't. First of all, she's too fat to reach around to her back with her tongue or with a paw. Second of all—maybe this should be first of all—those quills would prick a bit. Would you like to clean thirty thousand needles with your tongue?

So Pat waddles through the forest, ungroomed and unconcerned about the fact. Nobody's about to pick a fight with her because she looks uncombed. Nobody's about to pick a fight with her anyway.

Pat's really not about to pick a fight with anyone either. Despite her scarecrow looks and her built-in swords, she's really pretty good-natured. She doesn't bother anyone, and she doesn't expect anyone to bother her. She's really rather shy; she prefers to go out at night and rest during the day. You may find her sleeping on her belly on the ground, or draped like an old shag carpet over a tree limb. If something wakes her up she might rattle her quills and chatter her teeth. I don't know if she's scared or if she thinks she's being fierce, but that's her quiet way of telling something to please go away. If she raises her quills and turns around, she can convince almost any hungry animal that it really didn't want porcupine meat for supper.

Speaking of supper, Pat likes to eat plants, leaves, flowers, fruit, vegetables, ax handles, boots (she doesn't like the laces), and potatoes. She's a strict vegetarian—wouldn't think of making supper out of another animal—but she does have a craving for salt. Anything that people may have perspired into or onto is fair game for her. That's why ax handles and boots may be included in her diet. She's got twenty-five feet of intestines loaded with parasites and bacteria to help her digest the questionable diet.

Pat does eat lots of bark from trees. She also likes to chew stems, branches and trunks of young trees. Some people think we should get rid of Pat because she gets carried away in her tree nibbling sometimes. When she chews in too far, the trees die. (However, I suspect that some of those people want to get rid of Pat because she's chewed one of their ax handles—with which they've cut down the trees.)

Other people say that we should keep Pat because she thins out a forest, makes room for other plants to grow, and drops food to animals that can't climb trees.

I say that this talk of getting rid of Pat or keeping her is a bunch of nonsense. She's a living creature, so she belongs.

Pat can only grunt, groan, cough, and whine, so she can't speak for herself. But I'm sure she'd agree with me. In fact, if the tables were turned and her animal friends were trying to decide whether or not they should keep us, Pat would probably put in a good grunt for us. And no one would dare to disagree with her.

21

Meet George

The first time I saw George, I thought his legs were much too long. So was his neck and his tongue. I had to admit that his soft brown eyes nearly melted my heart, and his long eyelashes almost made me jealous. But those little horns on top of his skinny head really did nothing for his appearance, and the brown spots all over his body left me completely baffled.

Of course, George wasn't human. George was a giraffe. I was just judging him by human standards, and found him lacking in almost every respect. But George didn't seem to mind at all. He was living by giraffe standards, and managing just fine.

George's legs were almost six feet long. I had

to look up to see the tops of his legs. It occurred to me that six-foot-long legs must be awfully heavy to move around. A lot of muscle can fit into six feet of legs. But I was using human standards again. We have muscles below our knees as well as above. Giraffes don't. Most of their leg muscles are in the upper parts of their legs. Their hoofs are controlled by elastic-like tendons. That's why George's legs looked skinny—no muscles on the bottom. This arrangement of muscles is convenient for a giraffe. One little twitch of a top muscle can send the whole leg swinging in a wide curve, sort of like a clock pendulum. For George's long legs, that's perfect.

Many animals, when they walk, put their right front foot and left back foot forward at the same time. It's a diagonal sort of affair that works well for them. George doesn't do this. His body is so short and his legs are so long that he'd run into trouble. His back foot might come forward and get all tangled up with his front foot. So George walks differently from most animals. His left front and left back feet move forward at the same time, then the right front and right back feet catch up. This way George doesn't stumble all over himself.

When George runs, he can reach speeds of about 35 miles an hour. He keeps his long tail twisted up over his back so that it doesn't get caught in any bushes while he's running.

How could anyone be happy with such a long neck? No one could, I guess, by human standards. For George, his neck is just fine. He likes to eat leaves from acacia trees in his African home, and that long neck gets his mouth right up to tender young leaves growing where no other animal can reach them. George gets a meal especially for him.

People have often wondered how George could live with such a long neck. It must take an awful lot of pressure to get his blood way up to his brain. Besides that, when he puts his head down to drink, his brain is about seven feet lower than his heart. The blood must almost rush down there and smother his brain. You'd think that when he raised his head quickly, the blood would rush away and he'd fall over in a dead faint. I know that if *I* stand up too fast I become giddy.

George, however, has a built-in system to take care of that problem. The main artery that brings blood to George's brain has muscle in the upper part of it. This muscle helps pump the blood all the way up his long neck to his brain. The vein that carries blood away from his brain is absolutely enormous. It has many one-way valves that won't allow the blood to flow in the wrong direction. So when George lowers his head to drink, the little valves do their work and keep the blood from rushing to his brain.

Besides that, George's long neck has very special joints. They are all ball-in-socket joints—the type we have connecting our arms to our bodies. This makes George's long neck very flexible. He can look in all directions without moving his body much at all.

A special tough, elastic-like tissue inside George's neck helps him keep it upright. You never see his neck sagging like a wet noodle.

George's head may look skinny and little to me, but it's perfect for him. It's connected to his neck by special bones in such a way that he can raise it almost straight up and down. He can almost bend it backwards over his neck. That helps when he's stretching for an especially tender acacia leaf.

George has holes in his head. Especially big sinuses, or hollows, in his head skeleton make his head very light, even for its small size. Could you imagine a great big elephant head atop that long, skinny neck?

His big brown eyes are placed far to the sides of his head, so that he can almost see behind himself without turning around. Besides that, his eyes are very sharp, so he can survey the whole area he's browsing in without much effort. To see as well and as far as George does, we would have to climb an 18-foot ladder and use a pair of binoculars.

George's long eyelashes help keep dust out of his eyes. He also has special muscles in his nostrils to close his nose and keep the dust outside where it belongs.

George's tongue isn't only long, it's also covered with rough skin. The insides of his lips are covered with bumps called papillae, and he always has lots of saliva in his mouth when he

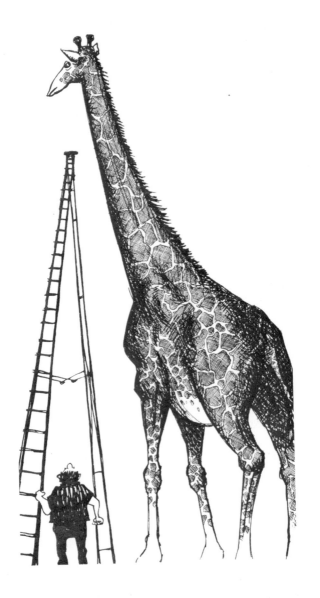

chews. None of this may sound very appetizing to us, but it surely helps protect George's mouth from thorns he happens to collect with the acacia leaves.

What about his horns? They look almost comical, with those little bumps on the ends. Actually, he should be proud of them; they're unique. Giraffes are the only animals born with horns. At first they're rather soft, but they soon begin changing to hard bone. They're not hollow, like cattle horns. They never fall off, like deer horns, or antlers. They're massive, solid bone, and they'll sit there throughout George's life. It's really good that they're knobbed at the end, because George uses them to fight other male giraffes for a female. Nobody gets hurt, because the knobs aren't sharp.

George, like all male giraffes, has extra-thick bone on the top of his skull, so his brain isn't rattled when he fights another male. Females don't have bone as thick; they also don't have knobs on their horns. That's okay, because females usually don't fight.

What about the spots? Different types of giraffes have different types of spots. George's just look like spots to me, but I can tell that his head and leg spots are smaller than his body spots. Some people say that spots help hide a giraffe when he's browsing in the trees. Other people say that isn't true. I don't know, but I think they're pretty—on a giraffe. I wouldn't want spots like that.

There I go, judging George by human standards again. True, a long neck, long legs, a long tongue, horns, and spots would look awful on a human. They just wouldn't do. But by George's standards they're just fine. If anybody ever asked me to make an animal, even in my imagination, I wouldn't come up with a giraffe. I guess I'm too limited by my human standards. I'm glad that God used giraffe standards when he made giraffes—and human standards when he made me.

22

My Magnificent Yacket

I have a jacket made of yak hair. I acquired it in Nepal. I love it, it's so warm and comfortable. I call it my magnificent yacket.

Every time I wear it I hope my friends will ask about it. I'd like to tell them how wonderful it is, and brag a little that it's made of yak hair. After all, there probably aren't many magnificent yackets in town.

The yak it came from is magnificent too. And there aren't many of them around either. Yaks live high in the desert steppes of Tibet. They flee from civilization, so they've been pushed higher and higher into smaller and smaller ranges.

Cold heights don't bother a yak. It's been created to live in cold, high places. Its coat is thick and matted on its head and back. Along its sides and shoulders hair hangs down like a mane. Even its tail is covered with thick hair and ends in a tassel. When a snowstorm roars through a yak's range, the animal simply turns its bushy tail into the wind and waits out the storm.

A type of wild ox closely related to our domestic cattle, the yak is a massive animal. A male yak can measure over ten feet long, seven feet high at the shoulder, and weigh over two thousand pounds. Its horns can be almost twenty inches across at the base and grow to over three feet long. Usually its horns are beautifully curved.

Its high territory (over sixteen thousand feet high) is dotted with marshes, swamps, and lakes. The yak has been created with special features for that country. It has long legs so that it can wade, rather than swim, through marshes. Its hoofs are extra large and wide so that it won't quickly sink in mucky soil. Its hoofs also have little extra claws which support the yak when it climbs in high mountains. Most oxen have thirteen pairs of ribs, but a yak has fourteen, giving its internal organs a little extra protection in case it takes a tumble down a rocky slope.

The country a yak lives in is too high to support trees and bushes. Only a few plants grow there. But a yak likes to eat herbs, swamp grass, and lichen, which do grow there.

In August and September the high country becomes hot and humid, at least for a yak, so it moves farther up to pastures which are always snow-covered. Somehow it finds lichen beneath the snow. It needs water, but has learned to eat snow when it's thirsty. Most of the time a yak likes to eat in the morning and evening, and lie down or bathe the rest of the day.

Yak mating season is in September. The big bulls will often fight each other for the cows. Sometimes they rip into each other's bodies with their long horns. But because the climate is cold and the air is quite pure, those wounds usually heal quickly.

A yak makes strange grunting sounds during the mating season. That's about the only noise it makes. The rest of the year it is not very vocal. Maybe that's how it acquired its scientific name: *Bos mutus,* the muted or quiet ox.

Old male yaks live singly or in small groups. (A yak is old at twenty-five years.) Young bulls live together in groups of about ten to twelve yaks. Females and their calves make up the biggest herds.

In the 1920s, many herds of thousands in each herd were counted in Tibet. In 1964 an estimated three thousand to eight thousand individuals remained. It is believed that their numbers are steadily dwindling today.

It's been twelve years since I traveled through yak territory and acquired my magnificent yacket. I've worn it for twelve years, and no one has asked me about it.

Maybe it isn't so magnificent. It's only a jacket that someone made. It isn't made perfectly. It really doesn't fit that well, and it always did look a little sloppy. It can always be replaced.

But a yak *is* a magnificent animal, created by God to fit perfectly where it lives. It can't be replaced.

23

The Incredible Hulks

The incredible hulk is here. Rather, the incredible hulks are *there*. People in the little town of Churchill in Manitoba, Canada have seen them. Several incredible hulks roam the streets there. One hulk ambled into the Legion Hall but was chased out because it wasn't a member. Another played hide-and-seek with law officers until it was caught in an abandoned bus. Another visits the town dump regularly.

They're not copies of the incredible hulk that used to star on TV once a week. They don't turn green and grow huge at the slightest irritation, as he does. They're white and they're always huge. They grunt and growl just like the TV incredible hulk, but they never talk. Yet they are hulks, and they are incredible. They're polar bears.

A big male polar bear can weigh up to 1,000 pounds. When he stands on his back legs he can be twelve feet tall, twice the size of an average man. He would be a match for the TV incredible hulk any time. And the polar bear doesn't shrink back to man-size the way our TV character did. He was created to grow big and stay big.

The TV incredible hulk outgrew his clothes whenever he became the hulk. Polar bears don't. They've been given beautiful fur coats that always fit them. Because they live in ice and snow, their fur is white with a tinge of yellow. That makes it difficult to see a polar bear walking on an ice pack. He looks more like a chunk of moving ice than like a bear.

The polar bear's coat is very thick and covers the bear completely to protect him from the cold weather. Long guard hairs lie on top of dense, fleecy underfur. As further insulation, a layer of fat covers the bear's whole body. This layer can be four inches thick. That's what makes the bear such a hulk.

Between the fat and the fur, a polar bear has a thin sheet of muscles that control blood vessels. When the bear is hot, it can open these blood vessels and bring blood closer to the skin to cool it off. When he's cold, it can close these vessels and keep his blood warm beneath the insulating fat.

A polar bear has long legs and broad paws that

help it move through deep snow faster than any other animal. Long claws and hair on the bottom of its paws give it a good grip on slippery ice. A polar bear can gallop over snow and ice at speeds up to 35 miles an hour.

The bear's toes are webbed to help it swim. With fat to help it float, a polar bear can swim nonstop for over a hundred miles if it must.

A polar bear has special eyes because it lives in such a white world. Even the TV incredible hulk wore sunglasses when the sun shone on the snow and ice. The polar bear, however, has built-in "sunglasses": an extra membrane covers its eyes and protects them from glare.

A polar bear's sense of smell is remarkable. This bear can scent a seal's breathing hole in the ice even if it's covered with four inches of snow. It needs this incredible sense of smell to help it hunt. A polar bear especially likes to eat seal meat. After it sniffs out a seal hole, the bear creeps up to it on its stomach and waits quietly. When the seal surfaces for air the bear strikes. One crunching blow from the bear's fifty-pound paw kills the seal instantly. Usually the bear will eat only the seal blubber. It leaves the rest of the meat for young bears unskilled at hunting, or for arctic foxes. The polar bear always washes its face and its paws carefully after it eats.

A female polar bear may have cubs every other year. About two months before the cubs are born, she'll dig a den inside a snowbank. It is big enough for her and her cubs. She punches a

little hole in the ceiling to let in light and fresh air. Sometimes she'll plug the main entrance with snow so that no one can find the den. Sometimes the winter blizzards will naturally plug the entrance.

A sloping entry tunnel helps conserve heat. Her own body warms the den. The den may be about forty degrees warmer than the air outside. It's a snug home for the cubs that will be born there.

A mother polar bear is devoted to her cubs for almost two years. When she introduces them to the white snowy world, she walks slowly so that the cubs can follow her. She stops often to let the cubs nurse or crawl on her back to warm their feet. She teaches them to hunt and to swim. Often she lets them cling to her tail if the swimming gets tough. She will attack anything that threatens her cubs. If you ever see a mother polar bear with cubs, keep your distance.

I don't suppose you'll see them, though, unless you live in Churchill or in the far north. Most residents of Churchill know how to treat polar bears—with great respect. People of Churchill are used to polar bears.

You see, Churchill grew up along an age-old polar bear migration route. The bears like to stay near ice, if possible. Every year they follow the Atlantic coast north for two or three hundred miles until they reach Cape Churchill, near the town of Churchill. The ice forms early at Cape

Churchill, and the bears seem to know that.

Every year, around November, Churchill residents have their own incredible hulks roaming the town. They were there long before the incredible hulk appeared on TV, and they are still there, long after he's been canceled. There's really no comparison between the TV man and the polar bears. After all, the TV incredible hulk was make-believe, thought up by some TV producer. The polar bears are real, incredible animals, created by God.